cooking with

PHILADELPHIA

Publications International, Ltd.

Louis Weber, CEO
Publications International, Ltd.
7373 North Cicero Avenue
Lincolnwood, IL 60712

Permission is never granted for commercial purposes.

TACO BELL® and *HOME ORIGINALS*® are trademarks owned and licensed by Taco Bell Corp.

Special thanks to *Kraft* Foods:
Brand Director: Nina Barton
Brand Team: Christopher Urban, Brant Wheaton, Jon Levy, and Kirtan Patel
Culinary Lead: Carrie Conway

For nutritional information, go to www.kraftrecipes.com.

Pictured on the front cover: Red Velvet Cupcakes *(page 230)*.

Pictured on the inside front cover: Fettuccine Primavera *(page 72)*.

Pictured on the back cover (clockwise from top): Marinated Cheese Cubes *(page 28)*, 20-Minute Skillet Salmon *(page 98)*, and Brown Sugar Cheesecake with Bourbon Sauce *(page 196)*.

Pictured on the inside back cover: Bacon & Maple Scalloped Potatoes *(page 158)*.

ISBN-13: 978-1-4508-6889-1
ISBN-10: 1-4508-6889-4

Library of Congress Control Number: 2013932296

Manufactured in China.

8 7 6 5 4 3 2 1

Microwave Cooking: Microwave ovens vary in wattage. Use the cooking times as guidelines and check for doneness before adding more time.

Preparation/Cooking Times: Preparation times are based on the approximate amount of time required to assemble the recipe before cooking, baking, chilling, or serving. These times include preparation steps such as measuring, chopping, and mixing. The fact that some preparations and cooking can be done simultaneously is taken into account. Preparation of optional ingredients and serving suggestions is not included.

CONTENTS

APPETIZERS...**4**   SIMPLE MEALS...**66**   ENTRÉES...**104**   SIDE DISHES...**148**
DESSERTS...**192**   HANDY TIPS...**246**   INDEX...**248**

APPETIZERS

MINI SALMON CAKES WITH CREAMY DILL SAUCE

PREP: 20 min. \ **TOTAL:** 1 hour 12 min. \ **MAKES:** 24 servings

- 1 tub (8 oz.) *Philadelphia* **Cream Cheese Spread, divided**
- 2 **Tbsp. chopped fresh dill**
- 1 **egg**
- 3 **green onions, sliced**
- 2 **Tbsp. chopped Italian parsley**
- 1 **Tbsp. lemon zest, divided**
- 1 **Tbsp. lemon juice, divided**
- 2 **cups flaked cooked salmon**
- 3 **Tbsp. milk**
- 1 **cup panko bread crumbs**
- ¼ **cup butter, melted**

1 **Heat** oven to 400°F.

2 **Mix** ½ cup cream cheese spread and next 4 ingredients in medium bowl. Stir in 1½ tsp. <u>each</u> lemon zest and juice. Add salmon; mix lightly. (Mixture will be moist.) Refrigerate 30 min. Meanwhile, whisk remaining cream cheese, lemon zest, juice and milk until well blended. Refrigerate until ready to serve.

3 **Mix** panko crumbs and butter in shallow dish. Roll salmon mixture into 48 balls, using 1 Tbsp. for each. Roll in crumb mixture until evenly coated; place, 1 inch apart, on baking sheet sprayed with cooking spray. Flatten slightly with fork.

4 **Bake** 20 to 22 min. or until each salmon cake is golden brown on both sides, turning after 10 min. Serve with cream cheese sauce.

SPECIAL EXTRA

For more flavor, add 1 Tbsp. capers to the salmon mixture before rolling into balls.

SALMON BITES

PREP: 10 min. \ **TOTAL:** 10 min. \ **MAKES:** 7 servings

---

7 slices dense pumpernickel bread

½ cup (½ of 8-oz. tub) *Philadelphia Cream Cheese Spread*

2 Tbsp. chopped fresh dill

3.5 oz. smoked salmon

1 **Use** 1¾-inch cookie cutter to cut 4 rounds out of each bread slice. Discard bread trimmings or reserve for another use.

2 **Mix** cream cheese spread with dill; spread over bread. Top with salmon.

SPECIAL EXTRA

Garnish each topped bread round with a sprig of fresh dill.

ROASTED SWEET POTATO & GARLIC SOUP

PREP: 30 min. \ **TOTAL:** 2 hours \ **MAKES:** 8 servings

2¼ lb. sweet potatoes (about 5), peeled, cut into 2-inch chunks

2 onions, chopped

1 head garlic, separated into cloves, peeled

2 Tbsp. olive oil

6 cups chicken broth

¼ cup (¼ of 8-oz. tub) *Philadelphia Cream Cheese Spread*

2 Tbsp. chopped fresh chives

1 **Heat** oven to 400°F.

2 **Toss** potatoes, onions and garlic with oil. Spread onto foil-covered baking sheet. Bake 1 hour or until vegetables are tender; spoon into large saucepan.

3 **Stir** in broth. Bring to boil on medium-high heat. Remove from heat; cool slightly. Add to blender, in batches, with cream cheese spread; blend until smooth. Return to saucepan.

4 **Cook** on medium heat until heated through, stirring occasionally. Serve topped with chives.

ZESTY STUFFED OLIVES

PREP: 10 min. \ **TOTAL:** 10 min. \ **MAKES:** 10 servings

½ cup (½ of 8-oz. tub) *Philadelphia* **Cream Cheese Spread**

20 **colossal black olives**

2 **Tbsp.** *Kraft* **Zesty Italian Dressing**

2 **Tbsp. chopped fresh parsley**

1 **Spoon** cream cheese spread into small resealable plastic bag. Press cream cheese into one of the bottom corners of bag. Cut off small piece from corner of bag. Squeeze cream cheese into centers of olives.

2 **Place** olives on serving plate. Drizzle with dressing. Sprinkle with parsley.

SPRING VEGGIE PIZZA APPETIZER

PREP: 15 min. \ **TOTAL:** 2 hours 58 min. \ **MAKES:** 32 servings

---

2 pkg. (8 oz. each) refrigerated crescent dinner rolls

1 tub (8 oz.) *Philadelphia* ⅓ Less Fat than Cream Cheese

½ cup *Miracle Whip* Dressing

1 tsp. dill weed

½ tsp. onion powder

1 cup <u>each</u> chopped sugar snap peas and quartered cherry tomatoes

½ cup <u>each</u> sliced radishes, chopped yellow peppers and shredded carrots

3 green onions, chopped

1 **Heat** oven to 375°F.

2 **Unroll** each package of dough into 2 rectangles. Press onto bottom and up sides of 15×10×1-inch pan to form crust, firmly pressing seams and perforations together to seal.

3 **Bake** 11 to 13 min. or until golden brown; cool.

4 **Mix** reduced-fat cream cheese, dressing and seasonings until blended; spread onto crust. Top with remaining ingredients. Refrigerate 2 hours.

FESTIVE FAVORITE LAYERED DIP

PREP: 10 min. \ **TOTAL:** 10 min. \ **MAKES:** 6 cups or 48 servings, 2 Tbsp. each

- 1 tub (8 oz.) *Philadelphia* Cream Cheese Spread
- ½ cup *Breakstone's* or *Knudsen* Sour Cream
- ¼ cup *Miracle Whip* Dressing
- 1 cup *Taco Bell* *Home Originals* Thick 'N Chunky Salsa
- 1 pkg. (8 oz.) *Kraft* Shredded Mozzarella Cheese
- 1 green pepper, finely chopped
- 2 tomatoes, chopped
- 2 green onions, chopped

1 **Mix** first 3 ingredients until blended; spread onto bottom of shallow bowl.

2 **Top** with layers of all remaining ingredients.

Taco Bell and *Home Originals* are trademarks owned and licensed by Taco Bell Corp.

MAKE AHEAD
Dip can be stored in refrigerator up to 2 hours before serving.

SERVING SUGGESTION
Serve with crackers.

MINI CHEESE BALLS

PREP: 15 min. \ **TOTAL:** 2 hours 15 min. \ **MAKES:** 18 servings

- **1 tub (8 oz.) *Philadelphia* Chive & Onion Cream Cheese Spread**
- **1 pkg. (8 oz.) *Kraft* Shredded Mozzarella Cheese**
- **4 slices cooked *Oscar Mayer* Bacon, finely chopped**
- **½ tsp. Italian seasoning**
- **½ tsp. garlic powder**
- **½ cup toasted *Planters* Walnuts, ground**

1 **Mix** cream cheese spread and mozzarella in medium bowl until blended. Stir in bacon and seasonings.

2 **Shape** into 54 balls, using 1 tsp. cheese mixture for each. Roll in nuts.

3 **Refrigerate** 2 hours.

BAKED CRAB RANGOON

PREP: 20 min. \ **TOTAL:** 40 min. \ **MAKES:** 12 servings

---

1 **can (6 oz.) crabmeat, drained, flaked**

4 **oz. (½ of 8-oz. pkg.)** *Philadelphia* **Neufchâtel Cheese, softened**

¼ **cup** *Kraft* **Light Mayo Reduced Fat Mayonnaise**

2 **green onions, thinly sliced**

12 **won ton wrappers**

1 **Heat** oven to 350°F.

2 **Mix** first 4 ingredients until blended.

3 **Line** each of 12 muffin cups sprayed with cooking spray with 1 won ton wrapper, allowing edge of wrapper to extend over top. Fill with crab mixture.

4 **Bake** 18 to 20 min. or until edges are golden brown and filling is heated through.

FOR CRISPIER RANGOONS

Bake won ton wrappers in muffin cups at 350°F for 5 to 7 min. or until lightly browned. Fill with crabmeat mixture and bake 6 to 8 min. or until filling is heated through.

CHICKEN & CRANBERRY BITES

PREP: 10 min. \ **TOTAL:** 25 min. \ **MAKES:** 24 servings

---

1 pkg. (17.3 oz.) frozen puff pastry (2 sheets), thawed

¾ cup (¾ of 8-oz. tub) *Philadelphia* Cream Cheese Spread

1½ cups chopped cooked chicken breasts

½ cup canned whole berry cranberry sauce

1 Heat oven to 425°F.

2 Roll out 1 pastry sheet on lightly floured surface into 12-inch square; cut into 12 smaller squares. Place in single layer on lightly floured baking sheet. Repeat with remaining pastry sheet.

3 Spoon 1½ tsp. cream cheese spread onto center of each pastry square. Top with chicken and cranberry sauce.

4 Bake 14 to 15 min. or until pasty is golden brown, rotating baking sheet after 7 min.

HOW TO CUT PUFF PASTRY

Use a pizza cutter to easily cut the pastry dough into squares.

FRUIT & NUT BITES

PREP: 10 min. \ **TOTAL:** 10 min. \ **MAKES:** 6 servings

12 **round butter crackers**

¼ **cup (¼ of 8-oz. tub)** *Philadelphia* **Cream Cheese Spread**

2 **Tbsp. apricot preserves**

2 **Tbsp.** *Planters* **Sliced Almonds, toasted**

1 Spread crackers with cream cheese spread; top with preserves.

2 Sprinkle with almonds.

SUBSTITUTE

Substitute hot pepper jelly for the apricot jam.

PESTO CROSTINI

PREP: 20 min. \ **TOTAL:** 20 min. \ **MAKES:** 16 servings

⅓ cup *Kraft* Italian Vinaigrette Dressing

3 cups fresh basil leaves

⅓ cup *Kraft* Grated Parmesan Cheese

32 baguette slices (¼ inch thick), toasted

1 tub (8 oz.) *Philadelphia* Cream Cheese Spread

¼ cup *Kraft* Grated Parmesan Cheese

1 Blend dressing, basil and ⅓ cup Parmesan in blender until smooth.

2 Spread toast slices with cream cheese spread, then basil mixture.

3 Sprinkle with ¼ cup Parmesan.

STORAGE KNOW-HOW

Wrap stems of basil in damp paper towel; place in resealable plastic bag and refrigerate up to 4 days. Or place the bunch, stem-ends down, in a glass of water; cover with a plastic bag and refrigerate as directed.

MARINATED CHEESE CUBES

PREP: 10 min. \ **TOTAL:** 1 hour 10 min. \ **MAKES:** 16 servings

---

- **1 pkg. (8 oz.) *Philadelphia* Cream Cheese**
- **½ cup *Kraft* Balsamic Vinaigrette Dressing**
- **2 Tbsp. chopped fresh parsley**
- **1 Tbsp. finely chopped red onions**
- **1 tsp. lime zest**
- **½ tsp. cracked black pepper**

1 Cut cream cheese into 32 pieces; place in shallow dish.

2 Mix remaining ingredients until blended.

3 Pour dressing mixture over cream cheese. Refrigerate 1 hour.

SERVING SUGGESTION
Serve with baguette slices or assorted crackers.

CREAMY MEDITERRANEAN SPREAD

PREP: 10 min. \ **TOTAL:** 10 min. \ **MAKES:** 3 cups or 24 servings, 2 Tbsp. each

1 pkg. (8 oz.) *Philadelphia* Cream Cheese, softened

1 jar (7 oz.) roasted red peppers, drained, chopped

1 pkg. (4 oz.) *Athenos* Traditional Crumbled Feta Cheese

½ cup chopped kalamata olives (about 40)

¼ cup *Kraft* Balsamic Vinaigrette Dressing

2 Tbsp. chopped fresh parsley

1 **Spread** cream cheese onto bottom of shallow dish.

2 **Combine** remaining ingredients; spoon over cream cheese.

SERVING SUGGESTION
Serve with crackers.

SALSA ROLL-UPS

PREP: 15 min. \ **TOTAL:** 15 min. \ **MAKES:** 9 servings

---

4 oz. (½ of 8-oz. pkg.) *Philadelphia* **Neufchâtel Cheese, softened**

3 Tbsp. *Taco Bell® Home Originals®* **Thick 'N Chunky Salsa**

2 spinach-flavored tortillas (6 inch)

½ cup shredded *Kraft* **Mexican Style 2% Milk Finely Shredded Four Cheese**

½ tsp. chili powder

1 **Mix** Neufchâtel and salsa; spread onto tortillas.

2 **Top** with shredded cheese and chili powder; roll up tightly.

3 **Cut** each roll-up into 9 slices.

Taco Bell® and *Home Originals®* are trademarks owned and licensed by Taco Bell Corp.

MAKE AHEAD

Prepare roll-ups as directed, but do not cut into slices. Tightly wrap each roll-up in plastic wrap. Refrigerate up to 4 hours. Slice just before serving.

SWEET 'N HOT CHEESE SPREAD

PREP: 5 min. \ **TOTAL:** 5 min. \ **MAKES:** 1¼ cups or 10 servings, 2 Tbsp. each

- **1 pkg. (8 oz.)** *Philadelphia* **Cream Cheese, softened**
- **3 Tbsp. apricot jam**
- **⅛ tsp. ground red pepper (cayenne)**
- **¼ cup** *Planters* **Slivered Almonds**

1 **Spread** cream cheese onto bottom of microwaveable quiche dish or pie plate.

2 **Top** with jam; sprinkle with pepper and nuts.

3 **Microwave** on HIGH 1 min. or until heated through.

SUBSTITUTE
Substitute orange marmalade for the apricot jam.

SERVING SUGGESTION
Serve with crackers.

RUSTIC CARMELIZED ONION TART

PREP: 10 min. \ **TOTAL:** 1 hour \ **MAKES:** 10 servings

- **4 slices *Oscar Mayer* Bacon, cut into 1-inch pieces**
- **1 large onion, thinly sliced**
- **1 ready-to-use refrigerated pie crust (½ of 14.1-oz. pkg.)**
- **1 pkg. (8 oz.) *Philadelphia* Cream Cheese, softened**
- **¼ cup *Breakstone's* or *Knudsen* Sour Cream**
- **½ cup *Kraft* 2% Milk Shredded Swiss Cheese**

1 Cook bacon in large skillet on medium-high heat 5 min. or just until bacon is crisp, stirring occasionally. Remove bacon from skillet with slotted spoon, reserving drippings in skillet. Drain bacon on paper towels; set aside. Add onions to drippings; cook 15 to 20 min. or until onions are caramelized, stirring frequently.

2 Heat oven to 400°F. Unroll pie crust on baking sheet. Mix cream cheese and sour cream; spread onto crust. Spoon onion mixture and bacon onto center of crust, leaving 2-inch border; top with Swiss cheese. Fold border over filling, leaving opening in center and pleating crust as necessary to fit.

3 Bake 20 to 25 min. or until crust is lightly browned. Cool slightly.

SPECIAL EXTRA

For a touch of sweetness, add 1 Tbsp. orange marmalade to cooked onion mixture before spooning over cream cheese mixture on pie crust.

ARTICHOKE-CHEESE PUFFS

PREP: 10 min. \ **TOTAL:** 55 min. \ **MAKES:** 16 servings

---

36 round butter crackers, divided

1 pkg. (8 oz.) *Philadelphia* Cream Cheese, softened

¼ cup *Kraft* Grated Parmesan Cheese

¼ cup *Kraft* 2% Milk Shredded Mozzarella Cheese

½ cup chopped drained canned artichoke hearts

1 **Crush** 4 crackers; place crumbs in shallow dish. Mix cheeses and artichokes; shape into 32 balls, using 2 tsp. for each ball. Coat with crumbs; place in shallow pan. Refrigerate 30 min.

2 **Heat** oven to 350°F. Place remaining crackers in single layer on baking sheet; top each with 1 cheese ball.

3 **Bake** 15 min. or until heated through.

SPECIAL EXTRA

Add finely chopped red, green and yellow peppers to the crumbs before using to coat cheese balls as directed.

LAYERED SUN-DRIED TOMATO AND ARTICHOKE SPREAD

PREP: 10 min. \ **TOTAL:** 1 hour 10 min. \ **MAKES:** 1½ cups or 12 servings, 2 Tbsp. each

1 pkg. (8 oz.) *Philadelphia* Cream Cheese

3 Tbsp. finely chopped sun-dried tomatoes in oil, well drained

3 Tbsp. finely chopped drained canned artichoke hearts

2 Tbsp. pesto

2 Tbsp. chopped *Planters* Smoked Almonds

2 tsp. chopped fresh parsley

1 **Cut** cream cheese horizontally into 3 slices using dental floss. (See Tip.) Place 1 slice on large sheet of plastic wrap; top with tomatoes and second cream cheese slice.

2 **Combine** artichokes and pesto; spoon over second cream cheese layer.

3 **Top** with remaining cream cheese slice, nuts and parsley; press nuts and parsley lightly into cream cheese to secure. Wrap with plastic wrap. Refrigerate 1 hour.

HOW TO CUT CREAM CHEESE WITH DENTAL FLOSS

Wrap 18-inch piece of dental floss around bottom third of cream cheese overlapping ends. Pull ends steadily to cut cream cheese. Repeat to make a total of 3 slices.

SERVING SUGGESTION

Serve with crackers.

SAVORY THREE-CHEESE SPREAD

PREP: 9 min. \ **TOTAL:** 10 min. \ **MAKES:** 10 servings

- **1 pkg. (8 oz.)** *Philadelphia* **Cream Cheese, softened**
- **1 cup** *Kraft* **Shredded Cheddar Cheese**
- **3 slices** *Oscar Mayer* **Smoked Ham, finely chopped**
- **¼ cup** *Kraft* **Grated Parmesan Cheese**
- **1 Tbsp. chopped red bell peppers**
- **1 Tbsp. diagonally sliced green onions**
- **¼ tsp. ground red pepper (cayenne)**

1 **Spread** cream cheese onto bottom of 2½-cup microwaveable dish. Sprinkle with Cheddar cheese, ham and Parmesan cheese.

2 **Microwave** on HIGH 1 min. or until heated through.

3 **Top** with remaining ingredients.

SUBSTITUTE
Switch sliced jalapeño peppers, chopped roasted red peppers or *Taco Bell* *Home Originals* Thick 'N Chunky Salsa for any of the toppings for a different flavor combo.

Taco Bell and *Home Originals* are trademarks owned and licensed by Taco Bell Corp.

SERVING SUGGESTION
Serve with crackers.

HOLIDAY CHEESE TRUFFLES

PREP: 15 min. \ **TOTAL:** 3 hours 15 min. \ **MAKES:** 24 servings

---

2 pkg. (8 oz. each) *Philadelphia* **Cream Cheese, softened**

1 pkg. (8 oz.) *Kraft* **Shredded Cheddar Cheese**

1 tsp. garlic powder

Dash ground red pepper (cayenne)

¼ cup chopped roasted red peppers

2 green onions, chopped

1⅔ cups chopped *Planters* **Pecans**

1 **Beat** first 4 ingredients with mixer until blended. Divide in half. Add roasted peppers to half and onions to other half; mix each until blended.

2 **Refrigerate** several hours or until chilled.

3 **Shape** into 48 (1-inch) balls. Roll in nuts. Refrigerate until ready to serve.

CHEESE LOGS
Roll each half into 6-inch log before coating with nuts.

SERVING SUGGESTION
Serve with crackers.

CREAM CHEESE-BACON CRESCENTS

PREP: 15 min. \ **TOTAL:** 30 min. \ **MAKES:** 16 servings

1 **tub (8 oz.)** *Philadelphia* **Chive & Onion Cream Cheese Spread**

3 **slices** *Oscar Mayer* **Bacon, cooked, crumbled**

2 **cans (8 oz. each) refrigerated crescent dinner rolls**

1 **Heat** oven to 375°F.

2 **Mix** cream cheese spread and bacon until well blended.

3 **Separate** each can of dough into 8 triangles. Cut each triangle lengthwise in half. Spread each dough triangle with 1 generous tsp. cream cheese mixture. Roll up, starting at shortest side of triangle. Place, point-sides down, on baking sheet.

4 **Bake** 12 to 15 min. or until golden brown. Serve warm.

VARIATION

For a sweet version, prepare using *Philadelphia* Strawberry Cream Cheese Spread and substituting 3 Tbsp. chopped *Planters* Walnuts for the bacon.

EASY-BAKE CHEDDAR BISCUITS

PREP: 10 min. \ **TOTAL:** 22 min. \ **MAKES:** 9 servings

---

    1 cup flour

    2 tsp. *Calumet* Baking Powder

    ¼ tsp. cream of tartar

    ¼ tsp. sugar

    ¼ tsp. salt

    ¼ cup cold butter, cubed

    1 cup *Kraft* Shredded Cheddar Cheese

    ⅓ cup plus 2 Tbsp. milk

    ½ cup (½ of 8-oz. tub) *Philadelphia* Chive & Onion Cream Cheese Spread

1 Heat oven to 450°F.

2 Mix flour, baking powder, cream of tartar, sugar and salt in medium bowl. Cut in butter with pastry blender or 2 knives until mixture resembles coarse crumbs. Stir in Cheddar. Add milk; stir until mixture forms soft dough.

3 Place on lightly floured surface; knead 8 to 10 times or until smooth. Pat dough into 6-inch square; cut into 9 smaller squares. Place, 2 inches apart, on baking sheet.

4 Bake 10 to 12 min. or until golden brown. Cut in half; spread with cream cheese spread.

CARAMELIZED ONION & OLIVE TART

PREP: 40 min. \ **TOTAL:** 55 min. \ **MAKES:** 16 servings

- **2** large sweet onions, thinly sliced
- **3** Tbsp. *Kraft* Balsamic Vinaigrette Dressing
- **1** frozen puff pastry sheet (½ of 17.3-oz. pkg.), thawed
- **½** cup (½ of 8-oz. tub) *Philadelphia* Cream Cheese Spread
- **½** cup pitted kalamata olives, cut in half
- **¼** cup *Kraft* Grated Parmesan Cheese
- **1** Tbsp. chopped fresh thyme

1 Heat oven to 400°F.

2 Cook onions in dressing in large covered skillet on medium-low heat 25 min. or until tender, stirring occasionally. Remove from heat; set aside to cool.

3 Meanwhile, roll pastry into 12-inch square on lightly floured surface. Place in parchment-lined 15×10×1-inch pan. Spread with cream cheese spread to within 1 inch of edges; top with remaining ingredients.

4 Bake 15 min. or until pastry is golden brown. Serve warm or cooled to room temperature.

SUBSTITUTE

Prepare with phyllo dough instead. Layer 4 sheets of phyllo, brushing lightly with melted butter between the layers. Continue as directed, baking 18 to 20 min. or until golden brown.

COOL & CREAMY CRAB DIP

PREP: 15 min. \ **TOTAL:** 15 min. \ **MAKES:** 2 cups or 16 servings, 2 Tbsp. each

1 tub (8 oz.) *Philadelphia* Spinach & Artichoke Cream Cheese Spread

⅓ cup *Breakstone's* or *Knudsen* Sour Cream

1 can (6 oz.) crabmeat, drained, flaked

2 green onions, chopped

2 tsp. lemon juice

1 Mix cream cheese and sour cream in medium bowl until well blended.

2 Stir in remaining ingredients.

SERVING SUGGESTION
Serve with crackers and/or fresh vegetable dippers, such as pea pods.

SMOKED SALMON DIP

PREP: 10 min. \ **TOTAL:** 10 min. \ **MAKES:** 16 servings

---

1 tub (8 oz.) *Philadelphia* Cream Cheese Spread

⅓ cup *Kraft* Mayo Real Mayonnaise

⅓ cup *Breakstone's* or *Knudsen* Sour Cream

3 oz. smoked salmon, chopped (about ½ cup)

Grated zest from 1 lemon (about 1 Tbsp.)

1 Mix cream cheese spread, mayonnaise and sour cream until well blended.

2 Add salmon and lemon zest; stir gently until well blended.

JAZZ IT UP
Add 2 Tbsp. finely chopped fresh dill along with the salmon and lemon zest.

SERVING SUGGESTION
Serve with crackers.

CUCUMBER ROULADES

PREP: 10 min. \ **TOTAL:** 10 min. \ **MAKES:** 6 servings

- **1 English cucumber, peeled**
- **¼ cup (¼ of 8-oz. tub) *Philadelphia* Chive & Onion Cream Cheese Spread**
- **1 oz. smoked salmon, thinly sliced, cut into 12 pieces**
- **12 sprigs fresh dill**

1 Cut cucumber into 12 thick slices. Use melon baller to scoop out center of each.

2 Fill with cream cheese spread; top with salmon and dill.

SUBSTITUTE

Substitute 12 drained canned baby shrimp for the salmon.

WARM REUBEN SPREAD

PREP: 15 min. \ **TOTAL:** 35 min. \ **MAKES:** 2½ cups or 20 servings, 2 Tbsp. each

---

4 oz. (½ of 8-oz. pkg.) *Philadelphia* Cream Cheese, softened

½ cup *Kraft* Thousand Island Dressing

¼ lb. sliced deli corned beef, chopped (about 1 cup)

¾ cup well-drained *Claussen* Sauerkraut

1 pkg. (8 oz.) *Kraft* Big Slice Swiss Cheese Slices, chopped

1 Heat oven to 350°F.

2 Mix cream cheese and dressing in medium bowl until blended. Stir in remaining ingredients.

3 Spread onto bottom of 9-inch pie plate or shallow dish.

4 Bake 20 min. or until heated through.

SHORTCUT

Instead of baking prepared spread, microwave in microwaveable shallow dish on HIGH 2 to 3 min. or until heated through.

SERVING SUGGESTION

Serve with crackers.

PARTY CHEESE BALL

PREP: 15 min. \ **TOTAL:** 3 hours 15 min. \ **MAKES:** 3 cups or 24 servings, 2 Tbsp. each

---

- 2 pkg. (8 oz. each) *Philadelphia* Cream Cheese, softened
- 1 pkg. (8 oz.) *Kraft* Shredded Cheddar Cheese
- 1 Tbsp. finely chopped onions
- 1 Tbsp. chopped red peppers
- 2 tsp. Worcestershire sauce
- 1 tsp. lemon juice
- ¼ tsp. ground red pepper (cayenne)
- 1 cup chopped *Planters* Pecans, toasted

1 **Beat** cream cheese and Cheddar in small bowl with mixer until well blended.

2 **Add** all remaining ingredients except nuts; mix well. Refrigerate several hours.

3 **Shape** into ball; roll in nuts.

SERVING SUGGESTION

Serve with crackers.

HOT ONIONY CHEESE DIP

PREP: 25 min. \ **TOTAL:** 45 min. \ **MAKES:** 2¼ cups or 18 servings, 2 Tbsp. each

1 pkg. (8 oz.) *Philadelphia* Cream Cheese, softened

⅓ cup *Miracle Whip* Dressing

1 Tbsp. dry onion soup mix

1 cup *Kraft* Shredded Mozzarella Cheese

⅓ cup *Planters* Sliced Almonds, toasted

1 **Heat** oven to 350°F.

2 **Mix** first 3 ingredients in medium bowl. Stir in mozzarella.

3 **Spoon** into ovenproof serving dish.

4 **Bake** 15 to 20 min. or until heated through, stirring after 8 min. Top with nuts.

SERVING SUGGESTION

Serve with crackers and/or fresh vegetable dippers.

SAVORY PARMESAN BITES

PREP: 15 min. \ **TOTAL:** 30 min. \ **MAKES:** 32 servings

- **1 pkg. (8 oz.)** *Philadelphia* **Cream Cheese, softened**

- **1 cup** *Kraft* **Grated Parmesan Cheese, divided**

- **2 cans (8 oz. each) refrigerated crescent dinner rolls**

- **1 cup chopped red peppers**

- **¼ cup chopped fresh parsley**

1 Heat oven to 350°F.

2 Beat cream cheese and ¾ cup Parmesan with mixer until well blended.

3 Separate dough into 8 rectangles; seal seams. Spread with cream cheese mixture; top with peppers and parsley. Fold each rectangle lengthwise into thirds to enclose filling; cut into 4 squares. Place, seam-sides down, on baking sheet; top with remaining Parmesan.

4 Bake 13 to 15 min. or until golden brown.

SIMPLE MEALS

VEGETABLE CHOWDER

PREP: 15 min. \ **TOTAL:** 45 min. \ **MAKES:** 8 servings, 1 cup each

- **2 Tbsp. oil**
- **1 small onion, chopped**
- **2 cloves garlic, minced**
- **1 carrot, peeled, chopped**
- **1 cup coarsely chopped cauliflower florets**
- **1 large potato, peeled, chopped**
- **2 cups fat-free reduced-sodium chicken broth**
- **2 cups milk**
- **½ cup frozen corn**
- **1 tub (8 oz.) *Philadelphia* Cream Cheese Spread**
- **2 Tbsp. chopped fresh dill**

1 Heat oil in large saucepan on medium-high heat. Add onions and garlic; cook and stir 2 to 3 min. or until crisp-tender. Add carrots, cauliflower and potatoes; cook and stir 3 min.

2 Stir in broth, milk and corn. Bring to boil; cover. Simmer on medium-low heat 8 to 10 min. or until vegetables are tender.

3 Add cream cheese spread and dill; cook and stir 5 min. or until cream cheese is melted. (Do not let soup come to boil.)

SPECIAL EXTRA

Garnish each serving with 1 tsp. additional chopped fresh dill, or chopped fresh chives.

HAM & CHEESE MORNING QUICHES

PREP: 15 min. \ **TOTAL:** 45 min. \ **MAKES:** 6 servings, 2 quiches each

---

12 **slices whole wheat bread**

4 **eggs**

½ **cup (½ of 8-oz. tub)** *Philadelphia* ⅓ **Less Fat than Cream Cheese**

1 **Tbsp. milk**

¼ **cup finely chopped** *Oscar Mayer* **Deli Fresh Honey Ham**

2 **green onions, sliced**

1 Heat oven to 400°F.

2 Use rolling pin to flatten each bread slice to 5-inch square. Cut out centers with 3½-inch round cookie cutter. Discard trimmings or reserve for another use. Press 1 bread circle onto bottom and up side of each of 12 greased muffin cups.

3 Bake 8 to 10 min. or until golden brown. Reduce oven temperature to 350°F. Beat 1 egg and reduced-fat cream cheese in medium bowl with wire whisk until well blended. Add remaining 3 eggs, the milk, ham and onions; mix well. Pour into bread cups.

4 Bake 18 to 20 min. or until filling in center of each cup is set. Serve warm.

FETTUCCINE PRIMAVERA

PREP: 30 min. \ **TOTAL:** 30 min. \ **MAKES:** 4 servings, 1½ cups each

8 oz. fettuccine, uncooked

1 Tbsp. oil

1 lb. fresh asparagus spears, trimmed, cut into 2-inch lengths

1 small zucchini, sliced

2 cloves garlic, minced

½ cup (½ of 8-oz. tub) *Philadelphia* Cream Cheese Spread

2 Tbsp. chopped fresh dill

¾ cup chicken broth

3 green onions, sliced

1 Tbsp. lemon juice

¼ tsp. black pepper

1 Cook pasta as directed on package, omitting salt. Meanwhile, heat oil in large nonstick skillet on medium-high heat. Add asparagus, zucchini and garlic; cook and stir 2 to 3 min. or until crisp-tender. Spoon vegetables to one side of skillet.

2 Add cream cheese spread, dill and broth to other side of skillet; cook and stir 3 to 4 min. or until cream cheese is melted. Add onions and lemon juice; stir to evenly coat all ingredients in skillet with sauce. Cook and stir 1 to 2 min. or until heated through.

3 Drain pasta; place in large bowl. Add vegetable mixture; mix lightly. Sprinkle with pepper.

SPECIAL EXTRA

Add cooked shrimp, smoked salmon or leftover flaked cooked salmon to skillet with the onions and lemon juice.

MEDITERRANEAN FRITTATA

PREP: 15 min. \ **TOTAL:** 55 min. \ **MAKES:** 6 servings

---

5 eggs, beaten

½ cup (½ of 8-oz. tub) *Philadelphia* ⅓ Less Fat than Cream Cheese

2 Tbsp. pesto

2 cloves garlic, minced

½ cup *Kraft* Shredded Mozzarella Cheese

1 zucchini, shredded

1 tomato, chopped

3 green onions, sliced

1 Heat oven to 350°F.

2 Mix all ingredients until well blended.

3 Spoon into greased 9-inch pie plate.

4 Bake 40 min. or until center is set. Let stand 5 min. before cutting into wedges to serve.

VARIATION

For a change of pace, substitute *Kraft* Shredded Swiss Cheese for the *Kraft* Shredded Mozzarella Cheese and 1 cup drained, canned stewed tomatoes for the chopped fresh tomato.

SPAGHETTI

PREP: 30 min. \ **TOTAL:** 30 min. \ **MAKES:** 4 servings, 1½ cups each

---

8 oz. spaghetti, uncooked

1 lb. extra-lean ground beef

2½ cups spaghetti sauce

4 oz. (½ of 8-oz. pkg.) *Philadelphia* Neufchâtel Cheese, cubed

2 Tbsp. *Kraft* Grated Parmesan Cheese

1 **Cook** spaghetti as directed on package, omitting salt.

2 **Meanwhile,** brown meat in large skillet. Stir in sauce and Neufchâtel; cook on low heat 3 to 5 min. or until sauce is well blended and heated through, stirring frequently.

3 **Drain** spaghetti. Add to sauce; mix lightly. Place on platter; top with Parmesan.

SPECIAL EXTRA

Sprinkle with chopped fresh basil or parsley before serving.

CHICKEN-PARMESAN BUNDLES

PREP: 35 min. \ **TOTAL:** 1 hour 5 min. \ **MAKES:** 6 servings

4 oz. (½ of 8-oz. pkg.) *Philadelphia* Cream Cheese, softened

1 pkg. (10 oz.) frozen chopped spinach, thawed, well drained

1¼ cups *Kraft* Shredded Low-Moisture Part-Skim Mozzarella Cheese, divided

6 Tbsp. *Kraft* Grated Parmesan Cheese, divided

6 small boneless skinless chicken breast halves (1½ lb.), pounded to ¼-inch thickness

1 egg

10 round butter crackers, crushed (about ⅓ cup)

1½ cups spaghetti sauce

1 Heat oven to 375°F.

2 Mix cream cheese, spinach, 1 cup mozzarella and 3 Tbsp. Parmesan until well blended; spread onto chicken breasts. Starting at one short end of each breast, roll up chicken tightly. Secure with wooden toothpicks, if desired.

3 Beat egg in pie plate. Mix remaining Parmesan and cracker crumbs in separate pie plate. Dip chicken, 1 at a time, in egg, then roll in crumb mixture. Place, seam-sides down, in 13×9-inch baking dish sprayed with cooking spray.

4 Bake 30 min. or until chicken is done, heating pasta sauce near the end of the chicken baking time. Discard toothpicks. Serve chicken topped with spaghetti sauce and remaining mozzarella.

SPECIAL EXTRA

Sprinkle with chopped fresh basil before serving.

POTATO-TOPPED MINI MEATLOAVES

PREP: 15 min. \ **TOTAL:** 40 min. \ **MAKES:** 6 servings

---

1 lb. extra-lean ground beef

1 pkg. (6 oz.) *Stove Top* Stuffing Mix

1 cup water

4 oz. (½ of 8-oz. pkg.) *Philadelphia* Cream Cheese, cubed

2 cloves garlic, minced

2 cups hot mashed potatoes

¼ cup chopped fresh parsley

1 jar (12 oz.) beef gravy, warmed

1 **Heat** oven to 375°F.

2 **Mix** meat, stuffing mix and water; press into 12 muffin cups sprayed with cooking spray.

3 **Bake** 20 to 25 min. or until done (160°F).

4 **Add** cream cheese and garlic to potatoes; stir until cream cheese is melted. Stir in parsley. Scoop over meatloaves. Serve with gravy.

CRISS-CROSS SHEPHERD'S PIE

PREP: 30 min. \ **TOTAL:** 58 min. \ **MAKES:** 8 servings

1½ **lb. Yukon Gold potatoes (about 3 large), peeled, cut into 1-inch chunks**

2 **cloves garlic**

2 **lb. extra-lean ground beef**

2 **onions, chopped**

2 **cups frozen corn**

1 **cup water**

1 **pkg. (1 oz.) onion soup mix**

1 **cup *Kraft* Shredded Cheddar Cheese**

¼ **cup (¼ of 8-oz. tub) *Philadelphia* Cream Cheese Spread**

1 **Heat** oven to 375°F.

2 **Cook** potatoes and garlic in boiling water in large saucepan 15 min. or until potatoes are tender. Meanwhile, brown meat with onions in large skillet; drain. Return to skillet. Stir in corn, water and soup mix; cook 3 min. or until water is absorbed, stirring frequently. Spoon into 8 ramekins.

3 **Drain** potatoes; return to saucepan. Add Cheddar and cream cheese spread; mash until potatoes are smooth and mixture is well blended. Spoon over meat mixture. Make decorative criss-cross or cross-hatch pattern by lightly dragging fork over potato layer.

4 **Bake** 15 to 20 min. or until heated through.

MAKE AHEAD

Assemble recipe as directed; cover with heavy-duty foil. Freeze up to 1 month. When ready to serve, thaw overnight in refrigerator. Bake, covered, 25 to 30 min. or until heated through, uncovering for the last 10 min.

CREAMY MUSTARD CHICKEN

PREP: 30 min. \ **TOTAL:** 30 min. \ **MAKES:** 4 servings

1 tsp. oil

4 small boneless skinless chicken breast
halves (1 lb.)

⅓ cup chicken broth

¼ cup (¼ of 8-oz. tub) *Philadelphia*
Cream Cheese Spread

1 Tbsp. *Grey Poupon* Harvest Coarse
Ground Mustard

1 Heat oil in large nonstick skillet on medium heat. Add chicken; cook 6 to 8 min. on each side or until done (165°F). Transfer to plate; cover to keep warm.

2 Add broth to skillet; cook on medium heat 3 to 5 min. or until hot. Add cream cheese spread and mustard; cook and stir 2 to 3 min. or until cream cheese is completely melted and sauce is well blended and slightly thickened.

3 Pour sauce over chicken.

SERVING SUGGESTION

Serve with potatoes, hot cooked rice or pasta and your favorite cooked vegetable.

CREAMY BASIL & RED PEPPER PASTA

PREP: 25 min. \ **TOTAL:** 25 min. \ **MAKES:** 4 servings

- **2 cups whole wheat penne pasta, uncooked**
- **1 jar (7 oz.) roasted red peppers, well drained**
- **4 oz. (½ of 8-oz. pkg.) *Philadelphia* Fat Free Cream Cheese, softened**
- **½ cup fat-free milk**
- **½ cup fresh basil**
- **2 Tbsp. *Kraft* Grated Parmesan Cheese**
- **1 lb. boneless skinless chicken breasts, cut into bite-size pieces**

1 Cook pasta as directed on package. Meanwhile, blend all remaining ingredients except chicken in blender until smooth.

2 Spray large skillet with cooking spray. Add chicken; cook on medium-high heat 3 min., stirring frequently. Stir in pepper mixture; simmer on medium heat 5 min. or until heated through, stirring frequently.

3 Drain pasta. Add to chicken mixture; mix lightly.

SPECIAL EXTRA

Garnish with additional fresh basil leaves.

CROQUE MONSIEUR

PREP: 5 min. \ **TOTAL:** 5 min. \ **MAKES:** 2 servings

- **2 slices French bread (1 inch thick)**
- **2 Tbsp. *Philadelphia* Chive & Onion Cream Cheese Spread**
- **12 slices *Oscar Mayer* Deli Fresh Virginia Brand Ham**
- **2 *Kraft* Big Slice Aged Swiss Cheese Slices**

1 Heat broiler.

2 Broil bread, 6 inches from heat, 30 sec. or until toasted; turn.

3 Spread with cream cheese spread; top with ham and Swiss cheese.

4 Broil 30 sec. or until Swiss cheese is melted.

SERVING SUGGESTION

Serve with a mixed green salad and your favorite fresh fruit to round out the meal.

FIESTA CHICKEN ENCHILADAS MADE OVER

PREP: 25 min. \ **TOTAL:** 45 min. \ **MAKES:** 4 servings

- **1 lb. boneless skinless chicken breasts, cut into bite-size pieces**
- **1 each large green and red pepper, chopped**
- **1 Tbsp. chili powder**
- **¾ cup *Taco Bell® Home Originals®* Thick 'N Chunky Salsa, divided**
- **2 oz. (¼ of 8-oz.-pkg.) *Philadelphia* Neufchâtel Cheese, cubed**
- **¾ cup *Kraft* Shredded Cheddar & Monterey Jack Cheeses, divided**
- **8 flour tortillas (8 inch)**

1. **Heat** oven to 375°F.

2. **Heat** large heavy nonstick skillet sprayed with cooking spray on medium heat. Add chicken, peppers and chili powder; cook and stir 8 min. or until chicken is done. Stir in ¼ cup salsa and Neufchâtel; cook and stir 3 to 5 min. or until Neufchâtel is melted and mixture is well blended. Stir in ¼ cup shredded cheese.

3. **Spoon** heaping ⅓ cup chicken mixture down center of each tortilla; roll up. Place, seam-sides down, in 13×9-inch baking dish sprayed with cooking spray; top with remaining salsa and shredded cheese. Cover.

4. **Bake** 20 min. or until heated through.

Taco Bell® and *Home Originals®* are trademarks owned and licensed by Taco Bell Corp.

VARIATION

Prepare using corn tortillas. To prevent cracking, warm tortillas as directed on package before using as directed.

ROAST PORK TENDERLOIN SUPPER

PREP: 20 min. \ **TOTAL:** 40 min. \ **MAKES:** 6 servings

---

2 pork tenderloins (1½ lb.)

¼ cup *Grey Poupon* Dijon Mustard

2 tsp. dried thyme leaves

1 pkg. (6 oz.) *Stove Top* Stuffing Mix for Chicken

½ cup chicken broth

4 oz. (½ of 8-oz. pkg.) *Philadelphia* Neufchâtel Cheese, cubed

1 lb. fresh green beans, trimmed, steamed

1 Heat oven to 400°F.

2 Heat large heavy nonstick skillet on medium heat. Add meat; cook 5 min. or until browned on all sides, turning occasionally. Transfer meat to 13✕9-inch baking dish, reserving drippings in skillet. Mix mustard and thyme; spread onto meat.

3 Bake 20 min. or until done (145°F). Transfer to carving board; tent with foil. Let stand 5 min. Meanwhile, prepare stuffing as directed on package, reducing margarine to 1 Tbsp.

4 Add broth to same skillet. Bring to boil on high heat. Add Neufchâtel; cook on medium-low heat 2 min. or until Neufchâtel is completely melted and sauce is well blended, stirring constantly.

5 Cut meat into thin slices. Serve topped with sauce along with the stuffing and beans.

NOTE

If you purchased the broth in a 32-oz. pkg., store remaining broth in refrigerator up to 1 week. Or, if you purchased a 14-oz. can, pour the remaining broth into a glass container; store in refrigerator up to 1 week.

ROASTED VEGGIE SANDWICH

PREP: 10 min. \ **TOTAL:** 22 min. \ **MAKES:** 2 servings

½ **red pepper**

2 **slices red onion (¼ inch thick)**

4 **slices <u>each</u> yellow squash and zucchini (¼ inch thick)**

⅛ **tsp. black pepper**

2 **squares focaccia bread (3 inch), split**

¼ **cup (¼ of 8-oz. tub) *Philadelphia* Spinach & Artichoke Cream Cheese Spread**

1 **Heat** oven to 400°F.

2 **Make** 2 or 3 small cuts in each short end of red pepper; press pepper to flatten. Place on baking sheet sprayed with cooking spray. Add remaining vegetables. Sprinkle with black pepper.

3 **Bake** 10 to 12 min. or until crisp-tender.

4 **Spread** cut sides of focaccia with cream cheese spread; fill with vegetables.

USE YOUR GRILL

Place grill pan on grill; heat on medium heat. Add vegetables to heated pan; brush with 1 Tbsp. olive oil. Grill 10 min. or until crisp-tender, turning after 5 min.

THREE-CHEESE CHICKEN PENNE PASTA BAKE

PREP: 25 min. \ **TOTAL:** 45 min. \ **MAKES:** 4 servings, 2 cups each

1½ cups multi-grain penne pasta, uncooked

1 pkg. (9 oz.) fresh baby spinach leaves

1 lb. boneless skinless chicken breasts, cut into bite-size pieces

1 tsp. dried basil leaves

1 can (14½ oz.) diced tomatoes, drained

1 jar (14 oz.) spaghetti sauce

2 oz. (¼ of 8-oz. pkg.) *Philadelphia* Neufchâtel Cheese, cubed

1 cup *Kraft* 2% Milk Shredded Mozzarella Cheese, divided

2 Tbsp. *Kraft* Grated Parmesan Cheese

1 **Heat** oven to 375°F.

2 **Cook** pasta in large saucepan as directed on package, omitting salt and adding spinach to the boiling water for last minute.

3 **Meanwhile,** heat large nonstick skillet sprayed with cooking spray on medium-high heat. Add chicken and basil; cook 3 min. or until chicken is no longer pink, stirring frequently. Stir in tomatoes and spaghetti sauce; bring to boil. Reduce heat to low; simmer 3 min. or until chicken is done. Add Neufchâtel; cook and stir until melted.

4 **Drain** pasta and spinach; return to same saucepan. Add chicken mixture; mix lightly. Stir in ½ cup mozzarella cheese. Spoon into 2-qt. or 8-inch square baking dish.

5 **Bake** 20 min. or until heated through. Sprinkle with remaining mozzarella and Parmesan cheeses. Bake 3 min. or until mozzarella is melted.

20-MINUTE SKILLET SALMON

PREP: 20 min. \ **TOTAL:** 20 min. \ **MAKES:** 4 servings

---

2 **Tbsp. oil**

4 **skin-on salmon fillets (1 lb.)**

1 **cup fat-free milk**

½ **cup (½ of 8-oz. tub)** *Philadelphia ⅓* **Less Fat than Cream Cheese**

½ **cup chopped cucumbers**

2 **Tbsp. chopped fresh dill**

1 Heat oil in large skillet on medium-high heat. Add fish; cook 5 min. on each side or until fish flakes easily with fork. Remove from skillet; cover to keep warm.

2 Add milk and reduced-fat cream cheese to skillet; cook and stir until cream cheese is melted and mixture is well blended. Stir in cucumbers and dill.

3 Return fish to skillet; cook 2 min. or until heated through. Serve topped with cream cheese sauce.

SPECIAL EXTRA

Garnish salmon with fresh dill sprigs before serving.

CREAMY ROSÉ PENNE

PREP: 20 min. \ **TOTAL:** 20 min. \ **MAKES:** 4 servings, 1¼ cups each

---

- **3 cups penne pasta, uncooked**
- **1½ cups spaghetti sauce**
- **⅓ cup (⅓ of 8-oz. tub) *Philadelphia Cream Cheese Spread***
- **¼ cup fresh basil**

1 Cook pasta as directed on package, omitting salt.

2 Meanwhile, heat spaghetti sauce in nonstick skillet on medium-high heat. Stir in cream cheese spread; cook and stir 2 to 3 min. or until melted.

3 Drain pasta; toss with sauce until evenly coated. Top with basil.

CREAMY POTATO-LEEK SOUP

PREP: 20 min. \ **TOTAL:** 1 hour \ **MAKES:** 10 servings, 1 cup each

2 **leeks, white and light green parts cut into 1-inch pieces**

2 **lb. Yukon Gold potatoes (about 8), peeled, cut into ½-inch cubes**

2 **Tbsp. *Kraft* Tuscan House Italian Dressing**

1 **Tbsp. chopped fresh rosemary**

3 **cups water**

1 **can (14½ oz.) chicken broth**

1 **pkg. (8 oz.) *Philadelphia* Cream Cheese, cubed, divided**

1 **Heat** oven to 400°F.

2 **Combine** vegetables, dressing and rosemary; spread onto baking sheet. Bake 35 to 40 min. or until vegetables are tender and golden brown, stirring occasionally.

3 **Place** water, broth and ¾ cup cream cheese cubes in large saucepan; cook on medium heat 3 min. or until mixture is well blended, stirring frequently with whisk. Stir in vegetables.

4 **Blend** soup, in batches, in blender until smooth. Return to saucepan; bring to boil. Thin soup with additional water, if desired. Serve topped with remaining cream cheese cubes.

SPECIAL EXTRA

Top with additional chopped fresh rosemary just before serving.

ENTRÉES

LASAGNA BAKE FOR TWO

PREP: 30 min. \ **TOTAL:** 50 min. \ **MAKES:** 2 servings

- **2 lasagna noodles, uncooked**
- **½ lb. extra-lean ground beef**
- **½ cup chopped onions**
- **1 clove garlic, minced**
- **1 cup (⅓ of 28-oz. can) undrained canned diced tomatoes**
- **2 Tbsp. *Philadelphia* Cream Cheese Spread**
- **4 cups loosely packed baby spinach leaves**
- **½ cup *Kraft* Finely Shredded Italian* Five Cheese Blend, divided**

1 Heat oven to 350°F.

2 Cook noodles as directed on package, omitting salt.

3 Meanwhile, brown meat with onions and garlic in large nonstick skillet. Add tomatoes and cream cheese spread; cook and stir 2 to 3 min. or until cream cheese is melted and mixture just comes to boil. Add spinach; cook and stir 1 min. Remove from heat. Add ¼ cup shredded cheese; stir until melted.

4 Drain noodles. Spoon ⅓ cup spinach mixture into each of 2 (2-cup) ramekins; top with noodle, letting excess noodle extend over rim of ramekin. Top each with ⅓ cup spinach mixture; fold noodle back over dish to cover filling. Repeat until all filling is folded between noodle layers; top with remaining shredded cheese.

5 Bake 20 min. or until heated through. Let stand 5 min. before serving.

*Made with quality cheeses crafted in the USA.

CREAMY TOMATO BAKED RIGATONI

PREP: 20 min. \ **TOTAL:** 55 min. \ **MAKES:** 6 servings, 1¼ cups each

---

8 oz. (½ of 16-oz. pkg.) rigatoni pasta, uncooked

2 cups spaghetti sauce

½ cup (½ of 8-oz. tub) *Philadelphia* Cream Cheese Spread

1 cup frozen broccoli florets, thawed

1 cup frozen cauliflower florets, thawed

1 cup *Kraft* Shredded Mozzarella Cheese, divided

⅓ cup fresh bread crumbs

2 Tbsp. margarine, melted

1 **Heat** oven to 350°F.

2 **Cook** pasta as directed on package, omitting salt. Meanwhile, microwave spaghetti sauce in large microwaveable bowl on HIGH 1½ to 2 min. or until hot. Add cream cheese spread; stir until well blended. Stir in vegetables and ½ cup mozzarella.

3 **Drain** pasta. Add to vegetable mixture; mix lightly. Spoon into 9-inch square baking dish sprayed with cooking spray. Combine remaining mozzarella, bread crumbs and margarine; sprinkle over pasta mixture.

4 **Bake** 30 to 35 min. or until casserole is heated through and top is golden brown.

HERB & GARLIC MEATBALLS

PREP: 40 min. \ **TOTAL:** 40 min. \ **MAKES:** 4 servings

1 **lb. extra-lean ground beef**

½ **cup dry bread crumbs**

½ **cup (½ of 8-oz. tub)** *Philadelphia* **Chive & Onion Cream Cheese Spread**

2 **Tbsp. oil**

2 **cups spaghetti sauce**

1 **cup water**

3 **cups hot cooked egg noodles**

1 **Mix** meat, bread crumbs and cream cheese spread until well blended; shape into 24 meatballs, using about 2 Tbsp. for each meatball.

2 **Heat** oil in large nonstick skillet on medium heat. Add meatballs; cook 5 to 6 min. or until evenly browned, turning occasionally. Drain fat from skillet, reserving meatballs in skillet. Add spaghetti sauce and water to skillet; stir to evenly coat meatballs. Simmer on medium-low heat 10 to 15 min. or until meatballs are done (160°F), stirring frequently.

3 **Serve** over noodles.

HOW TO SHAPE MEATBALLS

For evenly sized meatballs, use small ice cream scoop to portion meat mixture for each meatball.

FLORENTINE LINGUINE

PREP: 30 min. \ **TOTAL:** 30 min. \ **MAKES:** 4 servings, 1 cup each

8 oz. linguine, uncooked

1 Tbsp. olive oil

1 small onion, chopped

1 clove garlic, minced

½ cup (½ of 8-oz. tub) *Philadelphia Spinach & Artichoke Cream Cheese Spread*

½ cup chicken broth

½ cup milk

1 Cook pasta as directed on package, omitting salt.

2 Meanwhile, heat oil in large nonstick skillet on medium-high heat. Add onions and garlic; cook and stir 5 to 7 min. or until crisp-tender. Add cream cheese spread; cook and stir on medium heat 5 min. or until melted. Whisk in broth and milk; cook and stir 2 to 3 min. or until slightly thickened. (Do not boil.)

3 Drain pasta. Serve topped with sauce.

DEEP-DISH CHICKEN POT PIE

PREP: 20 min. \ **TOTAL:** 50 min. \ **MAKES:** 6 servings

- **1 lb. boneless skinless chicken breasts,** cut into 1-inch pieces
- **¼ cup** *Kraft* **Lite Zesty Italian Dressing**
- **4 oz. (½ of 8-oz. pkg.)** *Philadelphia* **Neufchâtel Cheese, cubed**
- **2 Tbsp. flour**
- **½ cup fat-free reduced-sodium chicken broth**
- **3 cups frozen mixed vegetables (peas, carrots, corn, green beans), thawed, drained**
- **1 ready-to-use refrigerated pie crust (½ of 14.1-oz. pkg.), thawed**

1 Heat oven to 375°F.

2 Cook chicken in dressing in large skillet on medium heat 2 min. Add Neufchâtel; cook and stir 3 to 5 min. or until melted. Stir in flour until well blended. Add broth and vegetables; stir. Simmer 5 min.

3 Pour into deep-dish 10-inch pie plate; cover with pie crust. Seal and flute edge. Cut slits in crust to permit steam to escape.

4 Bake 30 min. or until golden brown.

SUBSTITUTE

If a deep-dish pie plate is not available, you can use a 2-qt. round casserole instead.

BACON & TOMATO PRESTO PASTA

PREP: 20 min. \ **TOTAL:** 20 min. \ **MAKES:** 8 servings

---

8 slices *Oscar Mayer* **Bacon, chopped**

½ cup **cherry tomatoes**

1 tub (8 oz.) *Philadelphia* **Chive & Onion Cream Cheese Spread**

1 cup **milk**

½ cup *Kraft* **Grated Parmesan Cheese**

6 cups **hot cooked penne pasta**

1 **Cook** bacon in large skillet 5 min. or until bacon is crisp, stirring occasionally. Drain skillet, leaving bacon in skillet. Stir in tomatoes.

2 **Add** cream cheese spread, milk and Parmesan cheese; mix well. Cook until hot and bubbly, stirring frequently.

3 **Stir** in pasta.

SPECIAL EXTRA
Garnish with chopped fresh basil or parsley.

CREAMY BEEF STROGANOFF

PREP: 50 min. \ **TOTAL:** 50 min. \ **MAKES:** 4 servings

1 beef flank steak (1 lb.)

1 Tbsp. margarine

1 small onion, chopped

1 lb. sliced fresh mushrooms

2 bay leaves

1 tsp. chopped fresh thyme

1 can (14½ oz.) beef broth

½ cup (½ of 8-oz. tub) *Philadelphia Cream Cheese Spread*

¼ cup chopped fresh parsley

4 cups hot cooked egg noodles

1 Cook steak in large skillet on high heat 2 min. on each side or until browned on both sides. Remove from skillet; cover to keep warm.

2 Add margarine and onions to skillet; cook on medium heat 5 min. or until onions are crisp-tender, stirring occasionally. Stir in mushrooms, bay leaves and thyme; cook 10 min., stirring occasionally. Add broth; bring to boil. Simmer on low heat 3 min. or until slightly thickened. Add cream cheese spread; cook until melted, stirring frequently. Remove and discard bay leaves.

3 Cut steak across the grain into thin slices. Add to skillet; cook 3 to 5 min. or until meat is done. Stir in parsley. Serve over noodles.

VARIATION

Serve over hot cooked rice or mashed potatoes instead of the noodles.

QUICK & CREAMY CHICKEN STEW

PREP: 25 min. \ **TOTAL:** 25 min. \ **MAKES:** 4 servings, 1½ cups each

---

- ¾ **lb. new potatoes, quartered**
- 2 **Tbsp. water**
- 1 **Tbsp. oil**
- 1 **lb. boneless skinless chicken breasts, cut into bite-size pieces**
- 1 **can (10¾ oz.) reduced-fat reduced-sodium condensed cream of chicken soup**
- ¼ **cup *Kraft* Lite Zesty Italian Dressing**
- 2 **cups frozen peas and carrots**
- ½ **cup (½ of 8-oz. tub) *Philadelphia* Cream Cheese**

1 Place potatoes in microwaveable dish. Add water; cover with lid. Microwave on HIGH 7 min. or until potatoes are tender. Meanwhile, heat oil in large saucepan on medium-high heat. Add chicken; cook 7 min. or until evenly browned, stirring occasionally.

2 Add potatoes, soup, dressing and frozen vegetables to saucepan; stir. Bring to boil; cover. Simmer on medium-low heat 3 min. or until chicken is done and vegetables are heated through.

3 Stir in cream cheese; cook 3 min. or until melted, stirring occasionally.

SAUSAGE & PEPPERS LASAGNA

PREP: 30 min. \ **TOTAL:** 1 hour 30 min. \ **MAKES:** 12 servings

---

½ lb. Italian sausage

1 onion, chopped

½ cup <u>each</u> chopped green and red peppers

2 pkg. (8 oz. each) *Philadelphia* Cream Cheese, softened

½ cup milk

2½ cups *Kraft* Shredded Low-Moisture Part-Skim Mozzarella Cheese, divided

½ cup *Kraft* Grated Parmesan Cheese, divided

1 jar (24 oz.) spaghetti sauce

½ cup water

½ tsp. dried oregano leaves

12 lasagna noodles, cooked

1 **Heat** oven to 350°F.

2 **Brown** sausage with vegetables in large skillet. Meanwhile, beat cream cheese and milk in medium bowl with mixer until well blended. Combine mozzarella and Parmesan. Reserve 1½ cups. Add remaining to cream cheese mixture; mix well.

3 **Drain** sausage mixture; return to skillet. Stir in spaghetti sauce, water and oregano. Spread ⅓ of the meat sauce onto bottom of 13×9-inch baking dish; cover with 3 noodles and half the cream cheese mixture. Top with 3 noodles, half the remaining meat sauce and 3 noodles. Cover with layers of remaining cream cheese mixture, noodles, meat sauce and reserved cheese. Cover with foil sprayed with cooking spray.

4 **Bake** 1 hour or until heated through, uncovering after 45 min. Let stand 15 min. before cutting to serve.

VARIATION
Substitute extra-lean ground beef for the sausage and 1 thawed 10-oz. pkg. frozen chopped spinach for the peppers. Squeeze spinach to remove excess liquid before adding to cooked ground beef and onions with the spaghetti sauce and oregano.

CREAMY PASTA PRIMAVERA

PREP: 25 min. \ **TOTAL:** 25 min. \ **MAKES:** 6 servings, 1⅓ cups each

- **3** cups penne pasta, uncooked
- **2** Tbsp. *Kraft* Lite Zesty Italian Dressing
- **1½** lb. boneless skinless chicken breasts, cut into 1-inch pieces
- **2** zucchini, cut into bite-size chunks
- **1½** cups cut-up fresh asparagus (1-inch lengths)
- **1** red pepper, chopped
- **1** cup fat-free reduced-sodium chicken broth
- **4** oz. (½ of 8-oz. pkg.) *Philadelphia* Neufchâtel Cheese, cubed
- **¼** cup *Kraft* Grated Parmesan Cheese

1 Cook pasta in Dutch oven or large saucepan as directed on package.

2 Meanwhile, heat dressing in large skillet on medium heat. Add chicken and vegetables; cook 10 to 12 min. or until chicken is done, stirring frequently. Add broth and Neufchâtel; cook 2 min. or until Neufchâtel is melted, stirring constantly. Stir in Parmesan.

3 Drain pasta; return to pan. Add chicken mixture; mix lightly. Cook 1 min. or until heated through.

CREAMY CHICKEN, BACON & TOMATO PASTA

PREP: 20 min. \ **TOTAL:** 20 min. \ **MAKES:** 4 servings, 1¾ cups each

---

- **3 cups whole wheat farfalle (bow-tie pasta), uncooked**
- **1 lb. boneless skinless chicken breasts, cut into bite-size pieces**
- **3 slices cooked *Oscar Mayer* Bacon, crumbled**
- **1 can (14½ oz.) Italian-style diced tomatoes, undrained**
- **4 oz. (½ of 8-oz. pkg.) *Philadelphia* Neufchâtel Cheese, cubed**
- **½ cup water**
- **¼ tsp. black pepper**
- **3 Tbsp. *Kraft* Grated Parmesan Cheese**

1 Cook pasta as directed on package, omitting salt.

2 Meanwhile, cook chicken in large skillet on medium heat 5 to 6 min. or until chicken is done, stirring occasionally. Add next 5 ingredients; mix well. Cook 3 min. or until Neufchâtel is completely melted and mixture is well blended, stirring frequently.

3 Drain pasta; place in large bowl. Add sauce; mix lightly. Sprinkle with Parmesan.

PORK MEDALLIONS ALFREDO

PREP: 20 min. \ **TOTAL:** 20 min. \ **MAKES:** 4 servings, ¼ recipe each

- **1 pork tenderloin (1 lb.), cut into ½-inch-thick slices**
- **½ cup (½ of 8-oz. tub) *Philadelphia* Chive & Onion Cream Cheese Spread**
- **⅓ cup fat-free reduced-sodium chicken broth**
- **¼ cup *Kraft* Balsamic Vinaigrette Dressing**
- **1 cup frozen peas**
- **¼ cup *Kraft* Grated Parmesan Cheese**
- **1 Tbsp. lemon juice**
- **4 cups hot cooked egg noodles**
- **2 Tbsp. fresh basil, chopped**

1 Heat large heavy nonstick skillet on medium-high heat. Add meat; cook 2 min. on each side or until lightly browned on both sides.

2 Add cream cheese spread, broth and dressing; cook and stir 6 min. or until cream cheese is completely melted. Stir in peas, Parmesan and lemon juice; cook until meat is done and sauce is heated through, stirring frequently.

3 Serve over noodles; sprinkle with basil.

LINGUINE WITH SILKY MUSHROOM SAUCE

PREP: 20 min. \ **TOTAL:** 20 min. \ **MAKES:** 4 servings, 1¼ cups each

½ lb. linguine, uncooked

1 pkg. (½ lb.) sliced fresh mushrooms

½ cup fat-free reduced-sodium chicken broth

½ cup (½ of 8-oz. tub) *Philadelphia* Chive & Onion ⅓ Less Fat than Cream Cheese

2 cups baby spinach leaves

2 Tbsp. *Kraft* Grated Parmesan Cheese

Black pepper

1 **Cook** pasta as directed on package, omitting salt.

2 **Meanwhile,** heat skillet sprayed with cooking spray on medium-high heat. Add mushrooms; cook and stir 8 min. or until lightly browned. Add broth and reduced-fat cream cheese; cook and stir until cream cheese is melted and sauce is heated through. Add spinach; cook until just wilted, stirring frequently.

3 **Drain** pasta; toss with sauce. Sprinkle with Parmesan cheese and pepper.

SHORTCUT

Packaged sliced fresh mushrooms are available in the produce department of your grocery store.

ASPARAGUS BOW-TIE PASTA

PREP: 30 min. \ **TOTAL:** 30 min. \ **MAKES:** 4 servings, 1 cup each

---

- **2 cups farfalle (bow-tie pasta), uncooked**

- **1 lb. fresh asparagus spears, trimmed, cut into 1-inch lengths**

- **½ cup orange pepper strips**

- **¼ cup julienne-cut oil-packed sun-dried tomatoes, undrained**

- **½ cup chicken broth**

- **2 oz. (¼ of 8-oz. pkg.) *Philadelphia* Cream Cheese, cubed**

- **1 Tbsp. chopped fresh oregano**

- **1 cup *Kraft* Shredded Italian* Five Cheese Blend with a *Touch of Philadelphia***

1 **Cook** pasta in large saucepan as directed on package, omitting salt and adding asparagus to boiling water for the last 2 min. Drain.

2 **Meanwhile,** cook peppers and tomatoes in large skillet on medium-high heat 2 to 3 min. or until crisp-tender, stirring frequently.

3 **Add** pasta mixture, broth, cream cheese and oregano to skillet; mix well. Cook and stir 5 min. or until sauce is slightly thickened. Top with shredded cheese; cook 2 to 3 min. or until cheese begins to melt.

*Made with quality cheeses crafted in the USA.

SPECIAL EXTRA

Add 1½ cups cooked cleaned shrimp or chopped cooked chicken to skillet with the cooked pasta.

FISH IN ROASTED RED PEPPER SAUCE

PREP: 30 min. \ **TOTAL:** 30 min. \ **MAKES:** 4 servings

- **4** white fish fillets, such as tilapia or cod (1 lb.)
- **¼** cup flour
- **¼** cup *Kraft* Zesty Italian Dressing
- **½** cup sliced onions
- **2** oz. (¼ of 8-oz. pkg.) *Philadelphia* Cream Cheese, softened
- **¼** cup roasted fresh red peppers
- **¼** cup chicken broth
- **1** clove garlic
- **2** Tbsp. chopped fresh cilantro

1 **Coat** both sides of fish fillets with flour. Heat dressing in large skillet on medium-high heat. Add onions; cook and stir 5 min. or until crisp-tender. Add fish; cook 5 to 7 min. on each side or until fish flakes easily with fork.

2 **Meanwhile,** blend cream cheese, red peppers, broth and garlic in blender until smooth; pour into saucepan. Bring to boil on medium-high heat, stirring frequently; simmer on low heat 5 min., stirring occasionally.

3 **Serve** fish topped with cream cheese sauce and cilantro.

SUBSTITUTE

Substitute jarred roasted red peppers or roasted poblano peppers for the roasted fresh red peppers.

CURRY WITH PORK & PEPPERS

PREP: 30 min. \ **TOTAL:** 30 min. \ **MAKES:** 4 servings, 1¼ cups each

---

- **1 lb. pork tenderloin, cut into 1-inch pieces**
- **1 onion, cut into 1-inch pieces**
- **1 red pepper, cut into 1-inch pieces**
- **1 green pepper, cut into 1-inch pieces**
- **½ cup (½ of 8-oz. tub) *Philadelphia* Cream Cheese Spread**
- **1 Tbsp. Thai yellow curry paste**
- **½ cup coconut milk**
- **½ cup water**
- **2 cups hot cooked long-grain white rice**

1 Heat large skillet sprayed with cooking spray on medium-high heat. Add meat; cook and stir 4 min. or until evenly browned. Add vegetables; cook 4 to 6 min. or until vegetables are crisp-tender, stirring constantly.

2 Add cream cheese spread, curry paste, coconut milk and water; cook until cream cheese is melted, stirring constantly. Bring just to boil; simmer on medium-low heat 8 to 10 min. or until meat is done, stirring frequently.

3 Serve with rice.

SPECIAL EXTRA

Top with ¼ cup chopped fresh cilantro or toasted *Baker's Angel Flake* Coconut just before serving.

MEDITERRANEAN-STYLE STUFFED CHICKEN

PREP: 40 min. \ **TOTAL:** 1 hour 10 min. \ **MAKES:** 4 servings

- 4 oz. (½ of 8-oz. pkg.) *Philadelphia* Cream Cheese, softened
- 3 slices cooked *Oscar Mayer* Bacon, crumbled
- 2 Tbsp. dry bread crumbs
- 2 Tbsp. chopped kalamata olives
- 2 Tbsp. coarsely chopped *Planters* Slivered Almonds
- 1 egg
- 1 Tbsp. plus 1 tsp. chopped fresh thyme, divided
- 4 small boneless skinless chicken breast halves (1 lb.)
- 2 tsp. oil
- ½ cup dry white wine
- ½ cup chicken broth

1 **Heat** oven to 325°F.

2 **Combine** first 6 ingredients. Add 1 Tbsp. thyme; mix well. Use small sharp knife to cut pocket in thick long side of each chicken breast, being careful to not cut through to opposite side. Fill pockets with cream cheese mixture.

3 **Heat** oil in large skillet on medium-high heat. Add chicken; cook 3 to 4 min. on each side or until browned on both sides. Transfer to 13×9-inch baking dish sprayed with cooking spray; cover. Reserve drippings in skillet.

4 **Bake** 25 to 30 min. or until chicken is done (165°F). Meanwhile, add wine and broth to drippings; cook on medium heat 10 min. or until liquid is reduced by half, stirring frequently to scrape up browned bits from bottom of skillet. Stir in remaining thyme.

5 **Slice** chicken. Serve topped with sauce.

SERVING SUGGESTION
Serve with roasted butternut squash and purple cauliflower.

NON-ALCOHOLIC VARIATION
Omit wine. Increase chicken broth to 1 cup.

FISHERMAN'S CHOWDER

PREP: 40 min. \ **TOTAL:** 52 min. \ **MAKES:** 8 servings, 1 cup each

6 slices *Oscar Mayer* Bacon, chopped

1 large onion, chopped

2 stalks celery, chopped

1 large carrot, chopped

2 cups fat-free reduced-sodium chicken broth

1 large baking potato (8 oz.), cubed

½ cup (½ of 8-oz. tub) *Philadelphia* Cream Cheese Spread

2 cups milk

1 pkg. (14 oz.) frozen cod fillets, thawed, drained and cut into 2-inch pieces

1 Cook bacon in large saucepan until crisp, stirring occasionally. Use slotted spoon to remove bacon from pan, reserving 1 Tbsp. drippings in pan. Drain bacon on paper towels.

2 Add next 3 ingredients to drippings in pan; cook on medium heat 12 to 14 min. or until vegetables are crisp-tender, stirring occasionally. Add broth and potatoes; bring to boil. Cover; simmer 10 to 12 min. or until potatoes are tender.

3 Add cream cheese spread; cook, uncovered, 2 to 3 min. or until melted, stirring frequently. Add milk, fish and bacon; stir. Bring to boil, stirring frequently. Cook 3 to 4 min. or until fish flakes easily with fork.

MOZZARELLA-STUFFED CHICKEN BREASTS

PREP: 20 min. \ **TOTAL:** 50 min. \ **MAKES:** 4 servings, 1 stuffed chicken breast each

---

- 2 oz. (¼ of 8-oz. pkg.) *Philadelphia* Neufchâtel Cheese, softened

- ¼ cup finely chopped green peppers

- ½ tsp. dried oregano leaves

- ¼ tsp. garlic salt

- 1 cup *Kraft* Shredded Mozzarella Cheese, divided

- 4 small boneless skinless chicken breast halves (about 1 lb.), pounded to ¼-inch thickness

- 1 cup spaghetti sauce

1 **Heat** oven to 400°F.

2 **Mix** first 4 ingredients until well blended; stir in ½ cup mozzarella.

3 **Place** chicken, top-sides down, on work surface; spread with cheese mixture. Starting at one short end, tightly roll up each breast; place, seam-side down, in 8-inch square baking dish sprayed with cooking spray. Spoon spaghetti sauce over chicken; cover.

4 **Bake** 30 min. or until chicken is done (165°F). Sprinkle with remaining mozzarella; bake, uncovered, 3 to 5 min. or until melted.

GREEK CHICKEN WITH TZATZIKI SAUCE

PREP: 15 min. \ **TOTAL:** 45 min. \ **MAKES:** 4 servings

½ cup (½ of 8-oz. tub) *Philadelphia Cream Cheese Spread*

2 Tbsp. chopped fresh dill

6 Tbsp. milk

1 Tbsp. lemon juice

1 green onion, chopped

1 clove garlic, minced

1 lb. boneless skinless chicken breasts, cut into 1-inch pieces

¼ cup finely chopped English cucumbers

1 **Whisk** first 6 ingredients until well blended. Pour half over chicken in medium bowl; stir to evenly coat. Stir cucumbers into remaining sauce. Refrigerate both 20 min.

2 **Heat** grill to medium-high heat. Remove chicken from marinade; discard marinade. Thread chicken onto 8 skewers. Grill 8 to 10 min. or until chicken is done, turning occasionally.

3 **Serve** with tzatziki sauce.

SERVING SUGGESTION

Serve with hot cooked whole grains and your favorite vegetables.

CREAMY SHRIMP LINGUINE

PREP: 25 min. \ **TOTAL:** 25 min. \ **MAKES:** 4 servings, 1½ cups each

---

- 8 oz. linguine, uncooked
- 1 Tbsp. oil
- 1 lb. uncooked deveined peeled large shrimp
- 2 cloves garlic, minced
- ½ cup (½ of 8-oz. tub) *Philadelphia Cream Cheese Spread*
- 2 Tbsp. chopped fresh dill
- ¾ cup fat-free reduced-sodium chicken broth
- 1 Tbsp. lemon zest
- 2 cups snow peas, halved
- 1 cup cherry tomatoes, halved

1 **Cook** pasta as directed on package, omitting salt.

2 **Meanwhile,** heat oil in large nonstick skillet on medium-high heat. Add shrimp and garlic; cook and stir 3 to 5 min. or until shrimp turn pink. Remove from heat; cover to keep warm.

3 **Add** cream cheese spread, dill, broth and zest; cook and stir 2 to 3 min. or until cream cheese is melted and sauce is well blended. Add shrimp, snow peas and tomatoes; cook and stir 3 min. or until heated through.

4 **Drain** pasta. Add to shrimp mixture; toss to coat.

SIDE DISHES

MIXED GREEN SALAD WITH WARM CREAM CHEESE "CROUTONS"

PREP: 15 min. \ **TOTAL:** 15 min. \ **MAKES:** 8 servings, 1 cup each

---

4 oz. (½ of 8-oz. pkg.) *Philadelphia* Cream Cheese, cut into ½-inch cubes

¼ cup chopped *Planters* Sliced Almonds

8 cups torn salad greens

1 Granny Smith apple, thinly sliced

½ cup pomegranate seeds

⅓ cup *Kraft* Balsamic Vinaigrette Dressing

1 **Spray** large skillet with cooking spray; heat on medium heat. Meanwhile, coat cream cheese cubes with almonds.

2 **Add** cream cheese to skillet; cook 3 min. or until golden brown, turning occasionally.

3 **Combine** remaining ingredients in large bowl. Top with cheese. Serve immediately.

CREAMY SPINACH

PREP: 20 min. \ **TOTAL:** 20 min. \ **MAKES:** 4 servings, ²⁄₃ cup each

1 tsp. oil

½ small red onion, sliced

4 oz. (½ of 8-oz. pkg.) *Philadelphia Neufchâtel Cheese*, cubed

1 Tbsp. fat-free milk

¼ tsp. <u>each</u> salt and black pepper

2 pkg. (5 oz. each) baby spinach leaves

1 Heat oil in medium saucepan on medium-high heat. Add onions; cook and stir 3 to 4 min. or until crisp-tender.

2 Stir in Neufchâtel, milk and seasonings; cook and stir on low heat 1 to 2 min. or until Neufchâtel is melted and sauce is well blended.

3 Add ⅓ of the spinach; cook 2 min. or just until wilted, stirring frequently. Add remaining spinach, in batches, cooking and stirring after each addition just until wilted.

SPECIAL EXTRA
Cook ½ cup sliced fresh mushrooms with the onions.

CREAMY LEMON-ASPARAGUS RISOTTO

PREP: 20 min. \ **TOTAL:** 20 min. \ **MAKES:** 6 servings

2 **Tbsp. olive oil**

1 **medium onion, finely chopped**

2 **cups instant white rice, uncooked**

½ **lb. fresh asparagus spears, cut into 1-inch lengths**

2 **cups chicken broth**

2 **Tbsp. *Philadelphia* ⅓ Less Fat than Cream Cheese, softened**

Zest and juice from 1 lemon

1 **Heat** oil in large skillet on medium heat. Add onions; cook and stir 2 min. or until crisp-tender.

2 **Stir** in rice, asparagus and broth. Bring to boil. Reduce heat to low; simmer 5 min.

3 **Add** reduced-fat cream cheese, lemon zest and juice; cook until cream cheese is melted and mixture is well blended, stirring constantly.

SERVING SUGGESTION

Serve this risotto with grilled chicken or shrimp.

BUTTERNUT SQUASH PUFF

PREP: 10 min. \ **TOTAL:** 40 min. \ **MAKES:** 4 servings

¾ cup dry bread crumbs, divided

2 cups mashed cooked butternut squash

4 oz. (½ of 8-oz. pkg.) *Philadelphia* **Neufchâtel Cheese, softened**

2 Tbsp. brown sugar

1 egg

Dash <u>each</u> ground ginger, black pepper and salt

1 Heat oven to 350°F.

2 Reserve ¼ cup bread crumbs. Mix remaining crumbs with remaining ingredients until blended.

3 Spoon into 1-qt. casserole sprayed with cooking spray; sprinkle with reserved bread crumbs.

4 Bake 30 min. or until heated through.

BACON & MAPLE SCALLOPED POTATOES

PREP: 25 min. \ **TOTAL:** 1 hour 30 min. \ **MAKES:** 8 servings, 1 cup each

1 **red onion, thinly sliced**

4 **oz. (½ of 8-oz. pkg.)** *Philadelphia* **Cream Cheese, cubed**

1 **can (14½ oz.) fat-free reduced-sodium chicken broth**

½ **cup milk**

¼ **cup chopped** *Oscar Mayer* **Fully Cooked Bacon**

¼ **cup maple-flavored or pancake syrup**

2 **lb. Yukon Gold potatoes (about 8), cut into ¼-inch-thick slices**

1 **cup** *Kraft* **Shredded Triple Cheddar Cheese with a** *Touch of Philadelphia*

1 **Heat** oven to 400°F.

2 **Cook** onions in large skillet sprayed with cooking spray on medium-high heat 3 to 5 min. or until crisp-tender, stirring frequently. Remove onions from skillet.

3 **Add** cream cheese, broth and milk to skillet; cook and stir on medium-low heat 5 min. or until cream cheese is melted and mixture is well blended. Remove from heat; stir in bacon and syrup.

4 **Place** half the potatoes in 13×9-inch baking dish sprayed with cooking spray; cover with layers of onions and shredded cheese. Top with remaining potatoes and cream cheese sauce; cover.

5 **Bake** 1 hour 5 min. or until potatoes are tender and top is golden brown, uncovering after 50 min.

CREAMY VEGETABLE ORZO

PREP: 35 min. \ **TOTAL:** 35 min. \ **MAKES:** 6 servings, ½ cup each

---

- **1 Tbsp. oil**
- **1 small onion, chopped**
- **½ cup <u>each</u> chopped green and red peppers**
- **1 cup frozen corn**
- **¾ cup orzo pasta, uncooked**
- **1 can (14½ oz.) fat-free reduced-sodium chicken broth**
- **½ cup (½ of 8-oz. tub) *Philadelphia* Chive & Onion ⅓ Less Fat than Cream Cheese**

1 Heat oil in large skillet on medium heat. Add onions; cook 4 min., stirring frequently. Stir in peppers and corn; cook and stir 2 min. Add orzo; cook and stir 1 min.

2 Stir in broth; bring to boil on high heat. Simmer on medium-low heat 10 to 12 min. or until orzo and vegetables are tender and most of the liquid is absorbed, stirring occasionally.

3 Add reduced-fat cream cheese; cook 1 to 2 min. or until melted and sauce is well blended, stirring constantly.

SPECIAL EXTRA
Add 1 Tbsp. chopped fresh herbs, such as basil or rosemary, to the cooked vegetables with the broth.

ROASTED SWEET POTATO & CARROT PURÉE

PREP: 25 min. \ **TOTAL:** 1 hour 20 min. \ **MAKES:** 6 servings, ½ cup each

1 lb. sweet potatoes (about 2), peeled, cut into ½-inch pieces

8 carrots (about 1 lb.), peeled, cut into ½-inch-thick slices

3 Tbsp. olive oil

2 Tbsp. brown sugar

1 tsp. salt

1½ cups chicken broth, divided

4 oz. (½ of 8-oz. pkg.) *Philadelphia* Cream Cheese, cubed, softened

1 **Heat** oven to 375°F.

2 **Combine** first 5 ingredients; spread onto bottom of 15×10×1-inch pan. Pour 1 cup broth over vegetable mixture.

3 **Bake** 45 to 55 min. or until broth is absorbed and vegetables are tender and caramelized, stirring occasionally.

4 **Spoon** vegetables into food processor. Add remaining broth and cream cheese; process until smooth. Return to pan; cook 10 min. or until heated through, stirring frequently.

SPECIAL EXTRA

Before processing roasted vegetables in food processor, reserve ½ cup of the vegetables to use as a garnish for the finished dish.

CREAMY CITRUS-CHIVE ASPARAGUS

PREP: 15 min. \ **TOTAL:** 15 min. \ **MAKES:** 6 servings

---

2 **lb. fresh asparagus spears, trimmed**

1 **Tbsp. water**

¼ **cup fat-free reduced-sodium chicken broth**

½ **cup (½ of 8-oz. tub)** *Philadelphia* **Chive & Onion Cream Cheese Spread**

½ **tsp. lemon zest**

1 **Place** asparagus in microwaveable casserole. Add water; cover with waxed paper. Microwave on HIGH 4 to 5 min. or until asparagus is crisp-tender.

2 **Meanwhile,** heat broth in small saucepan. Add cream cheese spread; cook until cream cheese is melted and sauce is slightly thickened, stirring constantly. Stir in zest.

3 **Drain** asparagus; top with sauce.

SERVING SUGGESTION
Divide cooked asparagus spears into 6 bundles and tie each with a steamed green onion for a simple and elegant presentation.

CREAMY DOUBLE-MASHED POTATOES

PREP: 15 min. \ **TOTAL:** 35 min. \ **MAKES:** 6 servings, ¾ cup each

- **1 lb. sweet potatoes (about 2), peeled, cut into chunks**
- **1 lb. red potatoes (about 3), peeled, cut into chunks**
- **2 oz. (¼ of 8-oz. pkg.) *Philadelphia* Neufchâtel Cheese, cubed**
- **½ cup fat-free reduced-sodium chicken broth**
- **4 slices *Oscar Mayer* Bacon, cooked, crumbled**

1 Cook potatoes in boiling water in large saucepan 15 to 20 min. or until tender; drain. Return potatoes to pan.

2 Add Neufchâtel; mash potatoes just until blended. Gradually add broth, continuing to mash potatoes until of desired consistency.

3 Stir in bacon.

SUBSTITUTE

Substitute Yukon Gold potatoes for the red potatoes.

FABULOUS POTATOES

PREP: 20 min. \ **TOTAL:** 50 min. \ **MAKES:** 6 servings

- **2 lb. baking potatoes (about 6), peeled, cubed**

- **1 pkg. (8 oz.) *Philadelphia* Cream Cheese, cubed**

- **1 cup *Breakstone's* or *Knudsen* Sour Cream**

- **2 green onions, chopped**

1 Heat oven to 350°F.

2 Add potatoes to boiling water in saucepan; cook until tender. Drain.

3 Mash potatoes. Add cream cheese and sour cream; mash until fluffy. Spoon into greased 1-qt. casserole dish; cover.

4 Bake 30 min. or until heated through. Top with onions.

USE YOUR MICROWAVE

Mix all ingredients except onions as directed. Spoon into greased microwaveable 1-qt. casserole dish. Microwave on HIGH 8 to 10 min. or until heated through, stirring after 5 min. Top with onions.

CRUST-TOPPED BROCCOLI-CHEESE BAKE

PREP: 15 min. \ **TOTAL:** 45 min. \ **MAKES:** 14 servings

½ cup (½ of 8-oz. tub) *Philadelphia Chive & Onion Cream Cheese Spread*

1 can (10¾ oz.) condensed cream of mushroom soup

½ cup water

2 pkg. (16 oz. each) frozen broccoli florets, thawed, drained

1 cup *Kraft* Shredded Cheddar Cheese

1 frozen puff pastry sheet (½ of 17.3 oz. pkg.), thawed

1 egg, beaten

1 **Heat** oven to 400°F.

2 **Mix** cream cheese spread, soup and water in large bowl until blended. Stir in broccoli and Cheddar. Spoon into 2½- to 3-qt. shallow rectangular or oval baking dish.

3 **Roll** pastry sheet on lightly floured surface to fit top of baking dish. Cover dish completely with pastry. Press pastry edges against rim of dish to seal. Brush with egg; pierce with knife to vent.

4 **Bake** 30 min. or until filling is heated through and pastry is puffed and golden brown.

TWICE-BAKED SWEET POTATOES

PREP: 20 min. \ **TOTAL:** 55 min. \ **MAKES:** 4 servings

---

2 large sweet potatoes (1½ lb.)

2 oz. (¼ of 8-oz. pkg.) *Philadelphia Neufchâtel Cheese, cubed*

2 Tbsp. fat-free milk

1 Tbsp. brown sugar

¼ tsp. ground cinnamon

¼ cup chopped *Planters* Pecans

1 Heat oven to 425°F.

2 Cut potatoes lengthwise in half; place, cut-sides down, in foil-lined 15×10×1-inch pan. Bake 30 to 35 min. or until tender.

3 Scoop out centers of potatoes into bowl, leaving ¼-inch-thick shells. Add Neufchâtel, milk, sugar and cinnamon to potato flesh; mash until blended.

4 Fill shells with potato mixture; top with nuts. Bake 8 min. or until potatoes are heated through and nuts are toasted.

CROWD-PLEASING SCALLOPED POTATOES

PREP: 30 min. \ **TOTAL:** 2 hours \ **MAKES:** 18 servings

1 tub (8 oz.) *Philadelphia* Chive & Onion Cream Cheese Spread

2 cups fat-free reduced-sodium chicken broth

1 cup milk

10 slices *Oscar Mayer* Bacon, cooked, crumbled and divided

4½ lb. Yukon Gold potatoes (about 20), cut into ¼-inch-thick slices

1 onion, thinly sliced

1 cup *Kraft* 2% Milk Shredded Colby & Monterey Jack Cheeses

1 Heat oven to 400°F.

2 Cook first 3 ingredients in saucepan on medium heat until cream cheese spread is melted and mixture comes to boil, stirring constantly with whisk.

3 Reserve 2 Tbsp. bacon. Layer half <u>each</u> of the potatoes, onions and remaining bacon in 13×9-inch baking dish; repeat layers. Add cream cheese sauce; cover.

4 Bake 1½ hours or until potatoes are tender and top is golden brown, uncovering and topping with shredded cheese and reserved bacon the last 10 min.

EASY CARROT & BROCCOLI AU GRATIN

PREP: 25 min. \ **TOTAL:** 25 min. \ **MAKES:** 8 servings

---

 2 **cups baby carrots, cut in half**

 4 **cups small broccoli florets**

 10 **round butter crackers, crushed**

 3 **Tbsp.** *Kraft* **Grated Parmesan Cheese**

 1 **Tbsp. butter, melted**

 ¼ **lb.** *Velveeta*, **cut into ½-inch cubes**

 2 **oz. (¼ of 8-oz. pkg.)** *Philadelphia* **Cream Cheese, cubed**

1 Bring 3 cups water to boil in large saucepan on medium-high heat. Add carrots. Reduce heat to medium-low; simmer 8 min. Add broccoli; simmer an additional 3 min. or until vegetables are crisp-tender. Meanwhile, mix cracker crumbs, Parmesan and butter until blended.

2 Microwave *Velveeta* and cream cheese in microwaveable measuring cup or medium bowl on HIGH 1 min.; stir. Microwave 30 sec. or until *Velveeta* and cream cheese are completely melted and mixture is well blended when stirred.

3 Drain vegetables; place in serving bowl. Top with cheese sauce; sprinkle with crumb mixture.

SHORTCUT

Look for ¾-lb. packages of fresh broccoli florets in the produce section of your supermarket. Each bag contains about 4 cups which is just the amount you need to prepare this tasty recipe.

LEMON & PARSLEY BABY CARROTS

PREP: 30 min. \ **TOTAL:** 30 min. \ **MAKES:** 4 servings, ⅔ cup each

---

1 pkg. (1 lb.) baby carrots

1 cup water

⅓ cup chicken broth

4 oz. (½ of 8-oz. pkg.) *Philadelphia Neufchâtel Cheese, cubed*

1 tsp. lemon zest

1 Tbsp. chopped fresh parsley

1 Bring carrots and water to boil in medium saucepan on medium-high heat; cover. Cook 6 to 8 min. or until carrots are crisp-tender. Use slotted spoon to transfer carrots to bowl; reserve water in pan.

2 Return water to boil; cook 6 to 8 min. or until reduced by half. Add broth, Neufchâtel and zest; stir. Simmer on low heat 2 to 3 min. or until Neufchâtel is melted and sauce is well blended, stirring frequently. Stir in parsley.

3 Add carrots; toss to coat.

CREAMY TOMATO-CHICKEN RISOTTO

PREP: 45 min. \ **TOTAL:** 45 min. \ **MAKES:** 8 servings, 1¼ cups each

4 oz. 1½ of 8-oz. pkg.) *Philadelphia* **Cream Cheese, softened**

1 **can (28 oz.) diced tomatoes, drained, divided**

⅓ **cup** *Kraft* **Zesty Italian Dressing, divided**

1½ **lb. boneless skinless chicken breasts, cut into bite-size pieces**

1 **onion, chopped**

2 **carrots, chopped**

1½ **cups long-grain white rice, uncooked**

1 **jalapeño pepper, split, seeds and stem removed**

5½ **cups hot water, divided**

⅓ **cup finely chopped fresh cilantro**

1 Blend cream cheese and half the tomatoes in blender until smooth. Heat ¼ cup dressing in large skillet on medium heat. Add chicken; cook 6 min. or until done, stirring occasionally. Remove from skillet; cover to keep warm.

2 Cook onions, carrots and rice in remaining dressing in same skillet 3 min. or until rice is opaque, stirring frequently. Stir in jalapeño halves. Gradually add 1½ cups of the water; cook 5 min. or until water is completely absorbed, stirring occasionally. Repeat with the remaining water in batches, returning chicken to skillet with the last addition of water.

3 Stir in cream cheese mixture and remaining tomatoes; cook 3 min. or until heated through, stirring occasionally. Remove peppers; discard. Stir in cilantro.

BLT BRUSCHETTA

PREP: 20 min. \ **TOTAL:** 20 min. \ **MAKES:** 18 servings

- **1 French bread baguette (18 inch), ends trimmed, cut into 36 slices**
- **1 large clove garlic, peeled, cut in half**
- **¾ cup (¾ of 8-oz. tub) *Philadelphia* Cream Cheese Spread**
- **2 large plum tomatoes, chopped**
- **8 slices *Oscar Mayer* Bacon, cooked, crumbled**
- **1 cup chopped lettuce**
- **¼ cup *Kraft* Balsamic Vinaigrette Dressing**
- **⅓ cup *Kraft* Grated Parmesan Cheese**

1. **Heat** grill to medium heat.
2. **Grill** bread slices 2 min. on each side; cool.
3. **Rub** garlic onto toast; spread with cream cheese spread.
4. **Combine** tomatoes, bacon, lettuce and dressing; spoon over toast slices. Sprinkle with Parmesan.

SHORTCUT
Use pre-baked toast rounds purchased from the grocery store.

EASY BAKED CHEESE & VEGETABLE TWIST

PREP: 20 min. \ **TOTAL:** 1 hour \ **MAKES:** 16 servings

- 2 **eggs**
- 4 **oz. (½ of 8-oz. pkg.)** *Philadelphia* **Cream Cheese, softened**
- ½ **cup** *Kraft* **2% Milk Shredded Italian* Three Cheese Blend**
- 3 **cups frozen broccoli cuts, thawed, drained**
- ½ **lb. fresh mushrooms, cut into quarters**
- ½ **cup cherry tomatoes, cut in half**
- 4 **green onions, sliced**
- 2 **cans (8 oz. each) refrigerated crescent dinner rolls**

1 **Heat** oven to 375°F.

2 **Mix** first 3 ingredients in large bowl until well blended. Stir in next 4 ingredients.

3 **Unroll** crescent dough; separate into 16 triangles. Arrange in 11-inch circle on foil-covered baking sheet, with short sides of triangles overlapping in center and points of triangles toward outside. (There should be a 5-inch diameter opening in center of circle.) Spoon cheese mixture onto dough near center of circle. Bring outside points of triangles up over filling, then tuck under dough in center of ring to cover filling.

4 **Bake** 35 to 40 min. or until crust is golden brown and filling is heated through.

*Made with quality cheeses crafted in the USA.

SPECIAL EXTRA
Sprinkle with additional ½ cup shredded cheese before baking.

DIJON SCALLOPED POTATOES

PREP: 20 min. \ **TOTAL:** 1 hour 20 min. \ **MAKES:** 16 servings, ½ cup each

---

1 onion, chopped

6 oz. (¾ of 8-oz. pkg.) *Philadelphia* Cream Cheese, softened

1 can (14½ oz.) chicken broth

1 Tbsp. Dijon mustard

1½ lb. Yukon Gold potatoes (about 6), peeled, thinly sliced

60 round butter crackers, crushed (about 2 cups)

3 Tbsp. *Kraft* Grated Parmesan Cheese

2 Tbsp. butter, melted

2 tsp. chopped fresh parsley

1 Heat oven to 350°F.

2 Cook onions in large skillet sprayed with cooking spray on medium-high heat 5 to 7 min. or until crisp-tender, stirring frequently. Add cream cheese, broth and mustard; cook and stir 1 to 2 min. or until cream cheese is melted and sauce is well blended. Add potatoes; stir to evenly coat.

3 Spoon into 13×9-inch baking dish sprayed with cooking spray. Mix remaining ingredients; sprinkle over potatoes.

4 Bake 50 min. to 1 hour or until potatoes are tender.

SPECIAL EXTRA

For added color and flavor, substitute 1 sweet potato for 1 of the Yukon Gold potatoes.

CREAMED CORN

PREP: 10 min. \ **TOTAL:** 10 min. \ **MAKES:** 6 servings, ½ cup each

- 2 oz. (¼ of 8-oz. pkg.) *Philadelphia Cream Cheese*, cubed
- 2 Tbsp. milk
- 3 cups frozen whole kernel corn, thawed
- 1 can (14¾ oz.) cream-style corn
- ½ cup *Kraft* Shredded Cheddar Cheese
- ⅓ cup sliced green onions

1 Cook cream cheese and milk in medium saucepan on medium heat until cream cheese is melted, stirring frequently.

2 Add whole kernel corn and cream-style corn; stir. Cook 4 min. or until heated through, stirring occasionally.

3 Spoon into serving dish; sprinkle with Cheddar cheese and green onions.

SPECIAL EXTRA

If you like a hint of spice, stir in a dash or two of hot sauce.

EASY CAULIFLOWER & BROCCOLI AU GRATIN

PREP: 20 min. \ **TOTAL:** 20 min. \ **MAKES:** 10 servings, about ¾ cup each

5 **cups large broccoli florets**

4 **cups large cauliflower florets**

½ **cup water**

4 **oz. (½ of 8-oz. pkg.)** *Philadelphia* **Cream Cheese, softened**

¼ **cup milk**

½ **cup** *Breakstone's* **or** *Knudsen* **Sour Cream**

1½ **cups** *Kraft* **Shredded Sharp Cheddar Cheese**

10 **round butter crackers, crushed**

3 **Tbsp.** *Kraft* **Grated Parmesan Cheese**

1 **Place** broccoli and cauliflower in 2-qt. microwaveable dish. Add water; cover. Microwave on HIGH 8 to 10 min. or until vegetables are tender; drain. Set aside.

2 **Microwave** cream cheese and milk in 2-cup microwaveable measuring cup or medium bowl 1 min. or until cream cheese is melted and mixture is well blended when stirred. Add sour cream; mix well. Pour over vegetables; sprinkle with Cheddar cheese. Microwave 2 min. or until cheese is melted.

3 **Mix** cracker crumbs and Parmesan cheese. Sprinkle over vegetables.

NOTE
For best results, cut the broccoli and cauliflower into similarly sized pieces before microwaving.

DESSERTS

CHEESECAKE PARTY POPS

PREP: 30 min. \ **TOTAL:** 10 hours 45 min. \ **MAKES:** 42 servings

---

3 pkg. (8 oz. each) *Philadelphia* Cream Cheese, softened

¾ cup sugar

1 tsp. vanilla

2 eggs

8 oz. *Baker's* White Chocolate

8 oz. *Baker's* Semi-Sweet Chocolate

1 Heat oven to 325°F.

2 Line 13×9-inch pan with foil, with ends of foil extending over sides. Beat cream cheese, sugar and vanilla with mixer until well blended. Add eggs, 1 at a time, mixing after each just until blended. Pour into prepared pan.

3 Bake 35 min. or until center is set. Cool completely. Refrigerate 4 hours.

4 Use foil handles to lift cheesecake from pan before cutting into 42 squares. Roll each square into ball; place on parchment paper-covered baking sheet. Insert 1 lollipop stick into center of each. Freeze 4 hours.

5 Melt chocolates in separate bowls as directed on packages. Dip 21 lollipops in white chocolate; return to baking sheet. Repeat with remaining lollipops and semi-sweet chocolate. Drizzle remaining melted chocolate of contrasting color over lollipops. Refrigerate 1 hour or until chocolate is firm.

BROWN SUGAR CHEESECAKE WITH BOURBON SAUCE

PREP: 20 min. \ **TOTAL:** 6 hours 5 min. \ **MAKES:** 12 servings

¾ **cup butter, divided**

15 **chocolate sandwich cookies, finely crushed (about 1¼ cups)**

3 **pkg. (8 oz. each)** *Philadelphia* **Cream Cheese, softened**

1¾ **cups packed brown sugar, divided**

1 **Tbsp. vanilla**

3 **eggs**

½ **cup whipping cream**

¼ **cup bourbon**

1 **Heat** oven to 350°F.

2 **Melt** ¼ cup butter; mix with cookie crumbs until well blended. Press onto bottom of 9-inch springform pan.

3 **Beat** cream cheese, ¾ cup sugar and vanilla in large bowl with mixer until well blended. Add eggs, 1 at a time, beating on low speed after each just until blended. Pour over crust.

4 **Bake** 40 to 45 min. or until center is almost set. Run knife around rim of pan to loosen cake; cool completely before removing rim. Refrigerate 4 hours.

5 **Meanwhile,** bring cream, bourbon, remaining butter and sugar to boil in saucepan; simmer on medium-low heat 7 to 10 min. or until slightly thickened, stirring constantly. Cool. Refrigerate until ready to serve.

6 **Pour** bourbon sauce into microwaveable bowl. Microwave on HIGH 30 sec. or just until warmed; stir. Spoon 2 Tbsp. over each serving of cheesecake just before serving.

NON-ALCOHOLIC VARIATION

Substitute 2 tsp. vanilla for the bourbon.

MINT-CHOCOLATE CHEESECAKE

PREP: 20 min. \ **TOTAL:** 6 hours 8 min. \ **MAKES:** 16 servings

1¼ cups graham cracker crumbs

¼ cup butter, melted

3 pkg. (8 oz. each) *Philadelphia* Cream Cheese, softened

¾ cup sugar

3 eggs

1 tsp. mint extract

4 oz. *Baker's* Semi-Sweet Chocolate

½ cup whipping cream

1 **Heat** oven to 350°F.

2 **Mix** graham crumbs and butter; press onto bottom of 9-inch springform pan.

3 **Beat** cream cheese and sugar in large bowl with mixer until well blended. Add eggs, 1 at a time, beating on low speed after each just until blended. Stir in extract; pour over crust.

4 **Bake** 40 to 45 min. or until center is almost set. Run knife around rim of pan to loosen cake; cool before removing rim. Refrigerate 4 hours.

5 **Microwave** chocolate and cream in microwaveable bowl on MEDIUM (50%) 1 to 2 min. or until chocolate is almost melted; stir. Microwave 30 sec. to 1 min. or until chocolate is completely melted and mixture is well blended, stirring every 30 sec. Pour over cheesecake; let stand 5 to 10 min. or until glaze is firm.

SPECIAL EXTRA

For stronger mint flavor, increase the mint extract to 2 tsp.

CITRUS & RASPBERRY CHEESECAKE

PREP: 15 min. \ **TOTAL:** 6 hours \ **MAKES:** 16 servings

1¼ cups graham cracker crumbs

¼ cup butter, melted

3 pkg. (8 oz. each) *Philadelphia* **Cream Cheese, softened**

¾ cup granulated sugar

1 Tbsp. cornstarch

1 Tbsp. lemon zest

3 Tbsp. lemon juice

3 eggs

2 cups fresh raspberries

1 Tbsp. powdered sugar

1 Heat oven to 350°F.

2 Mix graham crumbs and butter; press onto bottom of 9-inch springform pan.

3 Beat cream cheese and granulated sugar in large bowl with mixer until well blended. Add cornstarch, zest and lemon juice; mix well. Add eggs, 1 at a time, beating on low speed after each just until blended. Pour over crust.

4 Bake 40 to 45 min. or until center is almost set. Run knife around rim of pan to loosen cake; cool before removing rim. Refrigerate 4 hours. Top with berries and powdered sugar just before serving.

SPECIAL EXTRA

Substitute 1 cup blueberries for 1 cup of the raspberries.

NEW YORK CHEESECAKE

PREP: 15 min. \ **TOTAL:** 5 hours 35 min. \ **MAKES:** 16 servings

---

- **1 cup graham cracker crumbs**
- **3 Tbsp. sugar**
- **3 Tbsp. butter, melted**
- **5 pkg. (8 oz. each) *Philadelphia* Cream Cheese, softened**
- **1 cup sugar**
- **3 Tbsp. flour**
- **1 Tbsp. vanilla**
- **1 cup *Breakstone's* or *Knudsen* Sour Cream**
- **4 eggs**
- **1 can (21 oz.) cherry pie filling**

1 Heat oven to 325°F.

2 Mix graham crumbs, 3 Tbsp. sugar and butter; press onto bottom of 9-inch springform pan. Bake 10 min.

3 Beat cream cheese, 1 cup sugar, flour and vanilla in large bowl with electric mixer on medium speed until well blended. Add sour cream; mix well. Add eggs, 1 at a time, mixing on low speed after each addition just until blended. Pour over crust.

4 Bake 1 hour 10 min. or until center is almost set. Run knife or metal spatula around rim of pan to loosen cake; cool before removing rim of pan. Refrigerate 4 hours. Top with pie filling before serving.

SPECIAL EXTRA

Omit cherry pie filling. Prepare and refrigerate cheesecake as directed. Top with 2 cups mixed berries. Brush with 2 Tbsp. strawberry jelly, melted.

NOTE

If using a dark nonstick 9-inch springform pan, reduce oven temperature to 300°F.

PUMPKIN-SWIRL CHEESECAKE

PREP: 20 min. \ **TOTAL:** 6 hours 25 min. \ **MAKES:** 16 servings

---

25 **gingersnap cookies, finely crushed (about 1½ cups)**

½ **cup finely chopped *Planters* Pecans**

¼ **cup butter, melted**

4 **pkg. (8 oz. each) *Philadelphia* Cream Cheese, softened**

1 **cup sugar, divided**

1 **tsp. vanilla**

4 **eggs**

1 **cup canned pumpkin**

1 **tsp. ground cinnamon**

¼ **tsp. ground nutmeg**

   Dash ground cloves

1 **Heat** oven to 325°F.

2 **Mix** cookie crumbs, nuts and butter; press onto bottom of 9-inch springform pan.

3 **Beat** cream cheese, ½ cup sugar and vanilla with mixer until blended. Add eggs, 1 at a time, beating after each just until blended. Remove 1 cup plain batter. Stir remaining sugar, pumpkin and spices into remaining batter.

4 **Spoon** half the pumpkin batter into crust; top with spoonfuls of half the plain batter. Repeat layers; swirl with knife.

5 **Bake** 55 min. to 1 hour 5 min. or until center is almost set. Run knife around rim of pan to loosen cake; cool before removing rim. Refrigerate cheesecake 4 hours.

BAVARIAN APPLE TORTE

PREP: 30 min. \ **TOTAL:** 4 hours 5 min. \ **MAKES:** 12 servings

---

½ **cup butter, softened**

1 **cup sugar, divided**

1 **cup flour**

1 **pkg. (8 oz.) *Philadelphia* Cream Cheese, softened**

1 **egg**

½ **tsp. vanilla**

½ **tsp. ground cinnamon**

4 **Granny Smith or Golden Delicious apples, peeled, sliced**

¼ **cup *Planters* Sliced Almonds**

1 **Heat** oven to 425°F.

2 **Beat** butter and ⅓ cup sugar in small bowl with electric mixer on medium speed until light and fluffy. Add flour; mix well. Spread onto bottom and 1 inch up side of 9-inch springform pan.

3 **Beat** cream cheese and ⅓ cup of the remaining sugar in same bowl with electric mixer on medium speed until well blended. Add egg and vanilla; mix well. Spread evenly over crust. Combine remaining ⅓ cup sugar and cinnamon. Add to apples in large bowl; toss to coat. Spoon over cream cheese layer; sprinkle with almonds.

4 **Bake** 10 min. Reduce temperature to 375°F; continue baking 25 min. or until center is set. Cool on wire rack. Loosen torte from rim of pan. Refrigerate 3 hours.

SUBSTITUTE

Substitute chopped *Planters* Pecans for the sliced almonds.

CHOCOLATE-VANILLA SWIRL CHEESECAKE

PREP: 15 min. \ **TOTAL:** 5 hours 25 min. \ **MAKES:** 16 servings

---

20 chocolate sandwich cookies, finely crushed (about 2 cups)

3 Tbsp. butter, melted

4 pkg. (8 oz. each) *Philadelphia* Cream Cheese, softened

1 cup sugar

1 tsp. vanilla

1 cup *Breakstone's* or *Knudsen* Sour Cream

4 eggs

6 oz. *Baker's* Semi-Sweet Chocolate, melted, cooled

1 **Heat** oven to 325°F.

2 **Mix** cookie crumbs and butter; press onto bottom of foil-lined 13×9-inch pan. Bake 10 min.

3 **Beat** cream cheese, sugar and vanilla in large bowl with mixer until well blended. Add sour cream; mix well. Add eggs, 1 at a time, mixing after each just until blended.

4 **Reserve** 1 cup batter. Stir chocolate into remaining batter; pour over crust. Top with spoonfuls of reserved batter.

5 **Swirl** batters with knife. Bake 40 min. or until center is almost set. Cool. Refrigerate 4 hours.

SPECIAL EXTRA

Garnish with chocolate curls just before serving. Use a vegetable peeler to shave the side of an additional 1 oz. *Baker's* Semi-Sweet Chocolate until desired amount of curls is obtained. Wrap remaining chocolate and store at room temperature for another use.

GINGERBREAD CHEESECAKE

PREP: 30 min. \ **TOTAL:** 6 hours 20 min. \ **MAKES:** 16 servings

22 **gingersnap cookies, finely crushed (about 1¼ cups)**

3 **Tbsp. butter, melted**

3 **pkg. (8 oz. each)** *Philadelphia* **Cream Cheese, softened**

¾ **cup sugar**

¼ **cup molasses**

1 **Tbsp. vanilla**

1 **tsp. ground cinnamon**

1 **tsp. ground nutmeg**

½ **tsp. ground ginger**

¼ **tsp. ground cloves**

3 **eggs**

4 **oz.** *Baker's* **Semi-Sweet Chocolate, chopped**

½ **cup whipping cream**

1 **Heat** oven to 350°F.

2 **Mix** cookie crumbs and butter; press onto bottom of 9-inch springform pan.

3 **Beat** cream cheese and sugar in large bowl with mixer until well blended. Add molasses, vanilla and spices; mix well. Add eggs, 1 at a time, mixing on low speed after each just until blended. Pour over crust.

4 **Bake** 45 to 50 min. or until center is almost set. Run knife around rim of pan to loosen cake; cool completely before removing rim. Refrigerate 4 hours.

5 **Microwave** chocolate and whipping cream in microwaveable bowl on HIGH 1 min.; stir. Microwave 30 sec to 1 min. or until chocolate is completely melted and mixture is well blended, stirring every 30 sec. Pour over cheesecake.

CHOCOLATE-RASPBERRY THUMBPRINTS

PREP: 20 min. \ **TOTAL:** 45 min. \ **MAKES:** 4½ doz. or 27 servings, 2 cookies each

---

2 cups flour

1 tsp. baking soda

¼ tsp. salt

4 oz. *Baker's* Unsweetened Chocolate

½ cup butter

1 pkg. (8 oz.) *Philadelphia* Cream Cheese, cubed, softened

1¼ cups sugar, divided

1 egg

1 tsp. vanilla

⅓ cup strawberry jam

1 Mix flour, baking soda and salt. Microwave chocolate and butter in large microwaveable bowl on HIGH 2 min.; stir until chocolate is completely melted. Add cream cheese; stir until blended. Stir in 1 cup sugar, egg and vanilla. Add flour; mix well. Refrigerate 15 min.

2 Heat oven to 375°F. Roll dough into 1-inch balls; coat with remaining sugar. Place, 2 inches apart, on baking sheets. Press your thumb into center of each ball; fill each indentation with about ¼ tsp. jam.

3 Bake 8 to 10 min. or until lightly browned. Cool 1 min. on baking sheets; transfer to wire racks. Cool completely.

SUBSTITUTE

Prepare using your favorite flavor of jam.

CHOCOLATE TURTLE CHEESECAKE

PREP: 15 min. \ **TOTAL:** 5 hours 50 min. \ **MAKES:** 16 servings

---

1½ cups crushed vanilla wafers (about 50)

¾ cup chopped *Planters* Pecans, divided

¼ cup butter, melted

32 *Kraft* Caramels

3 Tbsp. milk

4 pkg. (8 oz. each) *Philadelphia* Cream Cheese, softened

1 cup sugar

1 cup *Breakstone's* or *Knudsen* Sour Cream

4 eggs

8 oz. *Baker's* Semi-Sweet Chocolate, divided

1 Heat oven to 325°F.

2 Mix wafer crumbs, ½ cup nuts and butter; press onto bottom of 13×9-inch pan. Microwave caramels and milk in microwaveable bowl on MEDIUM (50%) 4 to 5 min. or until caramels are melted and mixture is well blended, stirring every 2 min. Pour over crust; spread to within 1 inch of edge. Cool.

3 Beat cream cheese and sugar with mixer until blended. Add sour cream; mix well. Add eggs, 1 at a time, mixing on low speed after each just until blended. Melt 7 oz. chocolate. Stir into cream cheese batter; pour over caramel layer.

4 Bake 45 to 50 min. or until center is almost set. Cool completely. Refrigerate 4 hours. Sprinkle with remaining nuts just before serving. Melt remaining chocolate; drizzle over cheesecake.

COOKING KNOW-HOW

For easy slicing, run a knife under hot water to warm up, then wipe dry before using to cut cheesecake. For best results, clean the knife after each slice.

DARK CHOCOLATE-HAZELNUT SOUFFLÉ

PREP: 10 min. \ **TOTAL:** 55 min. \ **MAKES:** 6 servings

---

1 tsp. butter

½ cup plus 1 Tbsp. sugar, divided

6 eggs

1 tub (8 oz.) *Philadelphia* **Cream Cheese Spread**

1 Tbsp. hazelnut-flavored liqueur

3 oz. *Baker's* **Bittersweet Chocolate, melted**

2 Tbsp. chopped hazelnuts, toasted

1 Heat oven to 350°F.

2 Grease bottom and side of 1-qt. soufflé dish with butter; sprinkle with 1 Tbsp. sugar.

3 Blend eggs, cream cheese spread, remaining sugar, liqueur and chocolate in blender 30 sec. or until smooth. Blend on high speed 15 sec. Pour into prepared dish.

4 Bake 40 to 45 min. or until puffed and lightly browned; sprinkle with nuts. Serve immediately.

SUBSTITUTE
Substitute a 1-qt. casserole dish for the soufflé dish.

VARIATION
Substitute 1 tsp. almond extract for the liqueur and *Planters* Slivered Almonds for the chopped hazelnuts.

LEMON-CREAM CHEESE CUPCAKES

PREP: 15 min. \ **TOTAL:** 1 hour 39 min. \ **MAKES:** 24 servings

1 pkg. (2-layer size) white cake mix

1 pkg. (3.4 oz.) *Jell-O* Lemon Flavor
  Instant Pudding

1 cup water

4 egg whites

2 Tbsp. oil

1 pkg. (8 oz.) *Philadelphia* Cream
  Cheese, softened

¼ cup butter, softened

2 Tbsp. lemon juice

1 pkg. (16 oz.) powdered sugar

1 **Heat** oven to 350°F.

2 **Beat** first 5 ingredients in large bowl with mixer on low speed 1 min. or until dry ingredients are moistened. (Batter will be thick.) Beat on medium speed 2 min. Spoon into 24 paper-lined muffin cups.

3 **Bake** 21 to 24 min. or until toothpick inserted in centers comes out clean. Cool in pans 10 min.; remove to wire racks. Cool completely.

4 **Beat** cream cheese, butter and lemon juice in large bowl with mixer until well blended. Gradually add sugar, beating well after each addition. Spread onto cupcakes.

SPECIAL EXTRA
Add 1 tsp. lemon zest to frosting before spreading onto cupcakes. Garnish each cupcake with a small twist of lemon zest.

NEAPOLITAN CHEESECAKE

PREP: 30 min. \ **TOTAL:** 6 hours 20 min. \ **MAKES:** 16 servings

---

1¼ cups graham cracker crumbs

¼ cup butter, melted

4 pkg. (8 oz. each) *Philadelphia* Cream Cheese, softened

1 cup sugar

4 eggs

2 oz. *Baker's* Semi-Sweet Chocolate, melted

1 Tbsp. vanilla

1 cup frozen strawberries, thawed, drained and mashed

2 oz. *Baker's* White Chocolate

1 **Heat** oven to 350°F.

2 **Mix** graham crumbs and butter; press onto bottom of 9-inch springform pan.

3 **Beat** cream cheese and sugar in large bowl with mixer until well blended. Add eggs, 1 at a time, mixing on low speed after each just until blended. Divide batter into thirds (about 2 cups each); pour each of 2 portions into separate small bowls. Stir semi-sweet chocolate into 1 portion, vanilla into second portion and berries into remaining portion.

4 **Pour** semi-sweet chocolate batter over crust; freeze 5 min. Cover with vanilla batter; freeze 5 min. Top with strawberry batter.

5 **Bake** 50 to 55 min. or until center is almost set. Run knife around rim of pan to loosen cake; cool completely before removing rim. Refrigerate 4 hours. Use vegetable peeler to make curls from white chocolate. Use to garnish cheesecake just before serving.

HOW TO MASH THE STRAWBERRIES
Use a potato masher or pastry blender to mash the strawberries.

CHOCOLATE ELEGANCE

PREP: 20 min. \ **TOTAL:** 4 hours 35 min. \ **MAKES:** 14 servings

---

1½ pkg. (8 oz. each) *Philadelphia* Cream Cheese (12 oz.), softened

½ cup sugar

2½ cups thawed *Cool Whip* Whipped Topping, divided

6 oz. *Baker's* Semi-Sweet Chocolate, divided

1 pkg. (3.9 oz.) *Jell-O* Chocolate Instant Pudding

½ cup cold milk

¼ cup *Planters* Sliced Almonds, toasted

1 **Beat** cream cheese and sugar with mixer until well blended. Stir in 1½ cups *Cool Whip*; spread 2 cups onto bottom of 8×4-inch loaf pan lined with plastic wrap.

2 Melt 3 oz. chocolate. Add to remaining cream cheese mixture along with dry pudding mix and milk; beat 2 min. Spread over layer in pan. Refrigerate 4 hours.

3 **Microwave** remaining chocolate and *Cool Whip* in microwaveable bowl on HIGH 1 min.; stir until blended. Cool slightly.

4 **Invert** dessert onto platter. Remove pan and plastic wrap. Spread dessert with glaze; top with nuts. Refrigerate until glaze is firm.

EASY DESSERT DIP

PREP: 5 min. \ **TOTAL:** 1 hour 5 min. \ **MAKES:** 1¾ cups or 14 servings, 2 Tbsp. each

1 pkg. (8 oz.) *Philadelphia* Cream Cheese, softened

1 jar (7 oz.) *Jet-Puffed* Marshmallow Creme

1 **Mix** ingredients until well blended.

2 **Refrigerate** 1 hour.

SERVING SUGGESTION

Serve with assorted cookies or cut-up fresh fruit.

NEW YORK-STYLE STRAWBERRY-SWIRL CHEESECAKE SQUARES

PREP: 20 min. \ **TOTAL:** 6 hours \ **MAKES:** 16 servings

- **1 cup graham cracker crumbs**
- **3 Tbsp. sugar**
- **3 Tbsp. butter, melted**
- **5 pkg. (8 oz. each) *Philadelphia* Cream Cheese, softened**
- **1 cup sugar**
- **3 Tbsp. flour**
- **1 Tbsp. vanilla**
- **1 cup *Breakstone's* or *Knudsen* Sour Cream**
- **4 eggs**
- **⅓ cup seedless strawberry jam**

1 Heat oven to 325°F.

2 Line 13×9-inch pan with foil, with ends of foil extending over sides. Mix graham crumbs, 3 Tbsp. sugar and butter; press onto bottom of pan. Bake 10 min.

3 Beat cream cheese, 1 cup sugar, flour and vanilla with mixer until well blended. Add sour cream; mix well. Add eggs, 1 at a time, mixing on low speed after each just until blended. Pour over crust. Drop small spoonfuls of jam over batter; swirl gently with knife.

4 Bake 40 min. or until center is almost set. Cool completely. Refrigerate 4 hours. Use foil handles to remove cheesecake from pan before cutting to serve.

CINNAMON TOAST "BLINIS"

PREP: 20 min. \ **TOTAL:** 35 min. \ **MAKES:** 18 servings, 2 rolls each

1 pkg. (8 oz.) *Philadelphia* **Cream Cheese, softened**

½ cup sugar, divided

¼ tsp. vanilla

1 egg yolk

1 tsp. ground cinnamon

12 slices white bread, crusts removed

3 Tbsp. butter, melted

1 Heat oven to 400°F.

2 Mix cream cheese, ¼ cup sugar, vanilla and egg yolk in medium bowl with wire whisk until well blended. In separate bowl, mix remaining ¼ cup sugar and cinnamon; set aside.

3 Flatten bread slices with rolling pin. Spread each with 1 rounded Tbsp. cream cheese mixture; roll up tightly, starting at one short end. Brush with butter; roll in reserved cinnamon sugar. Cut each roll into 3 pieces; place, seam-sides down, on baking sheet.

4 Bake 12 to 15 min. or until edges are lightly browned. Serve warm.

SPECIAL EXTRA

Prepare and bake rolls as directed. Dip each halfway into warmed *Baker's* Dipping Chocolate for an extra-special treat.

RED VELVET CUPCAKES

PREP: 15 min. \ **TOTAL:** 1 hour 15 min. \ **MAKES:** 24 servings

---

1 pkg. (2-layer size) red velvet cake mix

1 pkg. (3.9 oz.) *Jell-O* Chocolate Instant Pudding

1 pkg. (8 oz.) *Philadelphia* Cream Cheese, softened

½ cup butter or margarine, softened

1 pkg. (16 oz.) powdered sugar (about 4 cups)

1 cup thawed *Cool Whip* Whipped Topping

1 oz. *Baker's* White Chocolate, shaved into curls

1 Prepare cake batter and bake as directed on package for 24 cupcakes, blending dry pudding mix into batter before spooning into prepared muffin cups. Cool.

2 Beat cream cheese and butter in large bowl with mixer until well blended. Gradually beat in sugar. Whisk in *Cool Whip*. Spoon 1½ cups into small freezer-weight resealable plastic bag; seal bag. Cut small corner off bottom of bag. Insert tip of bag into top of each cupcake to pipe about 1 Tbsp. frosting into center of cupcake.

3 Frost cupcakes with remaining frosting; top with chocolate curls. Keep refrigerated.

STRAWBERRY-CHEESECAKE ICE CREAM

PREP: 20 min. \ **TOTAL:** 12 hours 20 min. \ **MAKES:** 8 servings, ½ cup each

- 1 pkg. (8 oz.) *Philadelphia* Cream Cheese, softened
- 1 can (14 oz.) sweetened condensed milk
- ⅓ cup whipping cream
- 2 tsp. lemon zest
- 1½ cups fresh strawberries
- 3 graham crackers, coarsely chopped

1 **Mix** first 4 ingredients with mixer until well blended. Freeze 4 hours or until almost solid.

2 **Beat** cream cheese mixture with mixer until creamy. Blend berries in blender until smooth. Add to cream cheese mixture with chopped grahams; mix well. Freeze 8 hours or until firm.

3 **Remove** ice cream from freezer 15 min. before serving; let stand at room temperature to soften slightly before scooping to serve.

PHILADELPHIA TRIPLE-CHOCOLATE CHEESECAKE

PREP: 20 min. \ **TOTAL:** 5 hours 45 min. \ **MAKES:** 16 servings

---

24 chocolate sandwich cookies, finely crushed (about 2 cups)

2 Tbsp. butter or margarine, melted

6 oz. *Baker's* White Chocolate, divided

4 pkg. (8 oz. each) *Philadelphia* Cream Cheese, softened, divided

1 cup sugar, divided

½ tsp. vanilla

3 eggs

3 oz. *Baker's* Semi-Sweet Chocolate, divided

1 tub (8 oz.) *Cool Whip* Whipped Topping, thawed

1 **Heat** oven to 325°F.

2 **Mix** cookie crumbs and butter; press onto bottom of 9-inch springform pan. Melt 5 oz. white chocolate as directed on package; cool slightly.

3 **Beat** 3 pkg. cream cheese, ¾ cup sugar and vanilla with mixer until well blended. Add melted white chocolate; mix well. Add eggs, 1 at a time, mixing on low speed after each just until blended. Pour over crust.

4 **Bake** 50 to 55 min. or until center is almost set. Run knife around rim of pan to loosen cake; cool completely. Meanwhile, melt 2 oz. semi-sweet chocolate; cool.

5 **Remove** rim of springform pan. Beat remaining cream cheese and sugar in large bowl until well blended. Add melted semi-sweet chocolate; mix well. Whisk in *Cool Whip*; spread over cheesecake. Refrigerate 4 hours. Garnish with chocolate curls made from remaining white and semi-sweet chocolates.

SIMPLY SENSATIONAL TRUFFLES

PREP: 20 min. \ **TOTAL:** 2 hours 20 min. \ **MAKES:** 3 doz. or 18 servings, 2 truffles each

20 oz. *Baker's* Semi-Sweet Chocolate, divided

1 pkg. (8 oz.) *Philadelphia* Cream Cheese, softened

Decorations: chopped *Planters* Cocktail Peanuts, multi-colored sprinkles

1 **Melt** 8 oz. chocolate as directed on package. Beat cream cheese in medium bowl with mixer until creamy. Blend in melted chocolate. Refrigerate 1 hour or until firm.

2 **Cover** baking sheet with waxed paper. Shape chocolate mixture into 36 balls, using about 2 tsp. for each. Place in single layer on prepared baking sheet.

3 **Melt** remaining chocolate. Use fork to dip truffles in chocolate; return to baking sheet. Decorate, then refrigerate 1 hour.

CREAMY LEMON NUT BARS

PREP: 15 min. \ **TOTAL:** 1 hour \ **MAKES:** 32 servings

½ cup butter, softened

⅓ cup powdered sugar

2 tsp. vanilla

1¾ cups flour, divided

⅓ cup chopped *Planters* Pecans

1 pkg. (8 oz.) *Philadelphia* Cream Cheese, softened

2 cups granulated sugar

3 eggs

1 Tbsp. lemon zest

½ cup lemon juice

1 Tbsp. powdered sugar

1 Heat oven to 350°F.

2 Line 13×9-inch baking pan with foil; spray with cooking spray. Mix butter, ⅓ cup powdered sugar and vanilla in large bowl. Gradually stir in 1½ cups flour and pecans. Press dough firmly onto bottom of prepared pan. Bake 15 min.

3 Beat cream cheese and granulated sugar in medium bowl with electric mixer on high speed until well blended. Add remaining ¼ cup flour and eggs; beat until blended. Stir in lemon zest and juice. Pour over crust.

4 Bake 30 min. or until center is set. Cool completely. Sprinkle with 1 Tbsp. powdered sugar just before serving.

SUBSTITUTE

Prepare as directed, using lime zest and lime juice.

BANANA SPLIT "CAKE"

PREP: 15 min. \ **TOTAL:** 5 hours 15 min. \ **MAKES:** 24 servings

---

1½ **cups graham cracker crumbs**

1 **cup sugar, divided**

⅓ **cup butter, melted**

2 **pkg. (8 oz. each)** *Philadelphia* **Cream Cheese, softened**

1 **can (20 oz.) crushed pineapple in juice, drained**

6 **bananas, divided**

2 **pkg. (3.4 oz. each)** *Jell-O* **Vanilla Flavor Instant Pudding**

2 **cups cold milk**

2 **cups thawed** *Cool Whip* **Whipped Topping, divided**

1 **oz.** *Baker's* **Semi-Sweet Chocolate, shaved into curls**

1 **Mix** graham crumbs, ¼ cup sugar and butter; press onto bottom of 13×9-inch pan. Freeze 10 min.

2 **Beat** cream cheese and remaining sugar with mixer until well blended. Spread carefully over crust; top with pineapple. Slice 4 bananas; arrange over pineapple.

3 **Beat** pudding mixes and milk in medium bowl with whisk 2 min. Stir in 1 cup *Cool Whip*; spread over banana layer in pan. Top with remaining *Cool Whip*. Refrigerate 5 hours.

4 **Slice** remaining bananas just before serving; arrange over dessert. Garnish with chocolate curls.

SUBSTITUTE

Substitute 1 cup chopped *Planters* Pecans for the shaved chocolate.

TIRAMISU BOWL

PREP: 20 min. \ **TOTAL:** 2 hours 20 min. \ **MAKES:** 16 servings, about ⅔ cup each

- 1 pkg. (8 oz.) *Philadelphia* Cream Cheese, softened
- 2 pkg. (3.4 oz. each) *Jell-O* Vanilla Flavor Instant Pudding
- 3 cups cold milk
- 1 tub (8 oz.) *Cool Whip* Whipped Topping, thawed, divided
- 48 vanilla wafers
- ½ cup brewed strong *Maxwell House* Coffee, cooled, divided
- 2 oz. *Baker's* Semi-Sweet Chocolate, grated
- 1 cup fresh raspberries

1 **Beat** cream cheese with mixer until creamy. Add dry pudding mixes and milk; beat 2 min. Gently stir in *Cool Whip*.

2 **Line** 2½-qt. bowl with 24 wafers; drizzle with ¼ cup coffee. Top with half <u>each</u> of the pudding mixture and chocolate. Repeat all layers.

3 **Top** with remaining *Cool Whip* and raspberries. Refrigerate 2 hours.

HOW TO EASILY GRATE CHOCOLATE
Before grating the chocolate, microwave it on HIGH for 10 sec. or just until slightly softened.

CREAMY LEMON SQUARES

PREP: 25 min. \ **TOTAL:** 3 hours 53 min. \ **MAKES:** 16 servings

20 reduced-fat vanilla wafers, finely crushed (about ¾ cup)

½ cup flour

¼ cup packed brown sugar

¼ cup cold margarine

1 pkg. (8 oz.) *Philadelphia* Neufchâtel Cheese, softened

1 cup granulated sugar

2 eggs

2 Tbsp. flour

3 Tbsp. lemon zest, divided

¼ cup fresh lemon juice

¼ tsp. *Calumet* Baking Powder

2 tsp. powdered sugar

1 **Heat** oven to 350°F.

2 **Line** 8-inch square pan with foil, with ends of foil extending over sides. Mix first 3 ingredients in medium bowl. Cut in margarine with pastry blender or 2 knives until mixture resembles coarse crumbs; press onto bottom of prepared pan. Bake 15 min.

3 **Meanwhile,** beat Neufchâtel and granulated sugar with mixer until well blended. Add eggs and 2 Tbsp. flour; mix well. Blend in 1 Tbsp. lemon zest, juice and baking powder; pour over crust.

4 **Bake** 25 to 28 min. or until center is set. Cool completely. Refrigerate 2 hours. Sprinkle with powdered sugar and remaining zest just before serving.

PHILADELPHIA Handy Tips

HOW TO SOFTEN CREAM CHEESE

- ► Place completely unwrapped package of cream cheese in microwaveable bowl.

- ► Microwave on HIGH 15 sec. or just until softened.

- ► Add 15 sec. for each additional package of cream cheese. Depending on the wattage of your microwave you may need to add more or less time.

HOW TO MEASURE CREAM CHEESE

- ► Each 8 oz. package of *PHILLY* brick or tub yields about 1 cup of cream cheese.

HOW TO STORE CREAM CHEESE AND CREAM CHEESE FROSTED CAKES

- ► Always store in refrigerator. For packages that have been opened, rewrap tightly in plastic wrap.

- ► Cakes filled and/or frosted with cream cheese frosting should be stored in the refrigerator.

- ► Freezing is not recommended.

HOW TO MELT CREAM CHEESE

PHILLY melts! Scoop a few spoonfuls of *PHILLY* tub or small cubes of *PHILLY* brick and follow these helpful hints to melt your *PHILLY* into sauces, soups, casseroles, and more.

- ► Add a few spoonfuls of *PHILLY* spread (or cubes of softened *PHILLY* brick) to warm sauce or soup and stir or whisk until cream cheese is completely melted.

- ► Add $1/2$ cup of *PHILLY* spread (or cubes of softened *PHILLY* brick) to a skillet containing $1/2$ to 1 cup of hot milk or broth. Stir or whisk constantly until cream cheese is melted. Add $1/2$ cup of *PHILLY* spread (or cubes of softened *PHILLY* brick) to 3 cups of hot cooked mashed potatoes and stir until combined.

HOW TO SUBSTITUTE ONE *PHILLY* FOR ANOTHER

- ► *PHILADELPHIA* Cream Cheese Flavored varieties add the same creamy flavorful richness to dishes as regular *PHILADELPHIA* Cream Cheese. Try varieties like *PHILADELPHIA* Chive & Onion or Sundried Tomato & Basil for a simple flavor twist.

- ► For all of the same great flavor and creaminess, but less fat than regular *PHILADELPHIA* Cream Cheese, *PHILADELPHIA* Neufchâtel Cheese can easily be substituted into your favorite dishes.

- ► In recipes, generally 4 oz. of cubed cream cheese is about equal to $1/2$ cup of cream cheese spread.

- ► It is not recommended to substitute *PHILADELPHIA* Cream Cheese Spreads (tub) in baked items like cheesecakes or breads.

INDEX

20-Minute Skillet Salmon **98**

Artichoke-Cheese Puffs **38**

Asparagus Bow-Tie Pasta **132**

Bacon & Maple Scalloped Potatoes **158**

Bacon & Tomato Presto Pasta **116**

Baked Crab Rangoon **20**

Banana Split "Cake" **240**

Bavarian Apple Torte **206**

BEEF & PORK

Bacon & Maple Scalloped Potatoes **158**

Bacon & Tomato Presto Pasta **116**

BLT Bruschetta **182**

Cream Cheese-Bacon Crescents **46**

Creamy Beef Stroganoff **118**

Criss-Cross Shepherd's Pie **82**

Croque Monsieur **88**

Crowd-Pleasing Scalloped Potatoes **174**

Curry with Pork & Peppers **136**

Ham & Cheese Morning Quiches **70**

Herb & Garlic Meatballs **110**

Lasagna Bake for Two **106**

Mini Cheese Balls **18**

Pork Medallions Alfredo **128**

Potato-Topped Mini Meatloaves **80**

Roast Pork Tenderloin Supper **92**

Rustic Carmelized Onion Tart **36**

Sausage & Peppers Lasagna **122**

Savory Three-Cheese Spread **42**

Spaghetti **76**

Warm Reuben Spread **58**

Chicken & Cranberry Bites **22**

CHICKEN & POULTRY

Chicken & Cranberry Bites **22**

Chicken-Parmesan Bundles **78**

Creamy Basil & Red Pepper Pasta **86**

Creamy Chicken, Bacon & Tomato Pasta **126**

Creamy Mustard Chicken **84**

Creamy Pasta Primavera **124**

Creamy Tomato-Chicken Risotto **180**

Deep-Dish Chicken Pot Pie **114**

Fiesta Chicken Enchiladas Made Over **90**

Greek Chicken with Tzatziki Sauce **144**

Mediterranean-Style Stuffed Chicken **138**

Mozzarella-Stuffed Chicken Breasts **142**

Quick & Creamy Chicken Stew **120**

Three-Cheese Chicken Penne Pasta Bake **96**

Chicken-Parmesan Bundles **78**

CHOCOLATE

Cheesecake Party Pops **194**

Chocolate Elegance **222**

BLT Bruschetta **182**

Brown Sugar Cheesecake with
    Bourbon Sauce **196**

Butternut Squash Puff **156**

Caramelized Onion & Olive Tart **50**

Cheesecake Party Pops **194**

Chocolate-Raspberry Thumbprints **212**

Chocolate Turtle Cheesecake **214**

Chocolate-Vanilla Swirl Cheesecake **208**

Dark Chocolate-Hazelnut Soufflé **216**

Gingerbread Cheesecake **210**

Mint-Chocolate Cheesecake **198**

Neapolitan Cheesecake **220**

Philadelphia Triple-Chocolate Cheesecake **234**

Red Velvet Cupcakes **230**

Simply Sensational Truffles **236**

Tiramisu Bowl **242**

Chocolate Elegance **222**

Chocolate-Raspberry Thumbprints **212**

Chocolate Turtle Cheesecake **214**

Chocolate-Vanilla Swirl Cheesecake **208**

Cinnamon Toast "Blinis" **228**

Citrus & Raspberry Cheesecake **200**

Cool & Creamy Crab Dip **52**

Cream Cheese-Bacon Crescents **46**

Creamed Corn **188**

Creamy Basil & Red Pepper Pasta **86**

Creamy Beef Stroganoff **118**

Creamy Chicken, Bacon & Tomato Pasta **126**

Creamy Citrus-Chive Asparagus **164**

Creamy Double-Mashed Potatoes **166**

Creamy Lemon-Asparagus Risotto **154**

Creamy Lemon Nut Bars **238**

Creamy Spinach **152**

Creamy Tomato Baked Rigatoni **108**

Creamy Tomato-Chicken Risotto **180**

Creamy Vegetable Orzo **160**

Criss-Cross Shepherd's Pie **82**

Croque Monsieur **88**

Crowd-Pleasing Scalloped Potatoes **174**

Crust-Topped Broccoli-Cheese Bake **170**

Cucumber Roulades **56**

Curry with Pork & Peppers **136**

Dark Chocolate-Hazelnut Soufflé **216**

Deep-Dish Chicken Pot Pie **114**

Dijon Scalloped Potatoes **186**

Easy-Bake Cheddar Biscuits **48**

Easy Baked Cheese & Vegetable Twist **184**

Easy Carrot & Broccoli au Gratin **176**

Easy Cauliflower & Broccoli au Gratin **190**

Easy Dessert Dip **224**

Fabulous Potatoes **168**

Festive Favorite Layered Dip **16**

Creamy Lemon Squares **244**

Creamy Mediterranean Spread **30**

Creamy Mustard Chicken **84**

Creamy Pasta Primavera **124**

Creamy Potato-Leek Soup **102**

Creamy Rosé Penne **100**

Creamy Shrimp Linguine **146**

Fettuccine Primavera **72**

Fiesta Chicken Enchiladas Made Over **90**

FISH & SEAFOOD

20-Minute Skillet Salmon **98**

Baked Crab Rangoon **20**

Cool & Creamy Crab Dip **52**

Creamy Shrimp Linguine **146**

Cucumber Roulades **56**

Fish in Roasted Red Pepper Sauce **134**

Fisherman's Chowder **140**

Mini Salmon Cakes with Creamy Dill Sauce **6**

Salmon Bites **8**

Smoked Salmon Dip **54**

Fish in Roasted Red Pepper Sauce **134**

Fisherman's Chowder **140**

Florentine Linguine **112**

Fruit & Nut Bites **24**

Gingerbread Cheesecake **210**

Greek Chicken with Tzatziki Sauce **144**

Ham & Cheese Morning Quiches **70**

Herb & Garlic Meatballs **110**

Holiday Cheese Truffles **44**

Hot Oniony Cheese Dip **62**

Lasagna Bake for Two **106**

Layered Sun-Dried Tomato and Artichoke Spread **40**

Lemon & Parsley Baby Carrots **178**

Lemon-Cream Cheese Cupcakes **218**

Linguine with Silky Mushroom Sauce **130**

Marinated Cheese Cubes **28**

Mediterranean Frittata **74**

Mediterranean-Style Stuffed Chicken **138**

Mini Cheese Balls **18**

Mini Salmon Cakes with Creamy Dill Sauce **6**

Mint-Chocolate Cheesecake **198**

Mixed Green Salad with Warm Cream Cheese "Croutons" **150**

Mozzarella-Stuffed Chicken Breasts **142**

Neapolitan Cheesecake **220**

New York Cheesecake **202**

New York-Style Strawberry-Swirl Cheesecake Squares **226**

Party Cheese Ball **60**

Pesto Crostini **26**

Philadelphia Triple-Chocolate Cheesecake **234**

Pork Medallions Alfredo **128**

Potato-Topped Mini Meatloaves **80**

Pumpkin-Swirl Cheesecake **204**

Quick & Creamy Chicken Stew **120**

Red Velvet Cupcakes **230**

Roast Pork Tenderloin Supper **92**

Roasted Sweet Potato & Carrot Purée **162**

Roasted Sweet Potato & Garlic Soup **10**

Roasted Veggie Sandwich **94**

Rustic Carmelized Onion Tart **36**

Salmon Bites **8**

Salsa Roll-Ups **32**

Savory Parmesan Bites **64**

Sausage & Peppers Lasagna **122**

Savory Three-Cheese Spread **42**

Simply Sensational Truffles **236**

Smoked Salmon Dip **54**

Spaghetti **76**

Spring Veggie Pizza Appetizer **14**

Strawberry-Cheesecake Ice Cream **232**

Sweet 'N Hot Cheese Spread **34**

Three-Cheese Chicken Penne Pasta Bake **96**

Tiramisu Bowl **242**

Twice-Baked Sweet Potatoes **172**

Vegetable Chowder **68**

Warm Reuben Spread **58**

Zesty Stuffed Olives **12**

METRIC CONVERSION CHART

VOLUME MEASUREMENTS (dry)

1/8 teaspoon = 0.5 mL
1/4 teaspoon = 1 mL
1/2 teaspoon = 2 mL
3/4 teaspoon = 4 mL
1 teaspoon = 5 mL
1 tablespoon = 15 mL
2 tablespoons = 30 mL
1/4 cup = 60 mL
1/3 cup = 75 mL
1/2 cup = 125 mL
2/3 cup = 150 mL
3/4 cup = 175 mL
1 cup = 250 mL
2 cups = 1 pint = 500 mL
3 cups = 750 mL
4 cups = 1 quart = 1 L

VOLUME MEASUREMENTS (fluid)

1 fluid ounce (2 tablespoons) = 30 mL
4 fluid ounces (1/2 cup) = 125 mL
8 fluid ounces (1 cup) = 250 mL
12 fluid ounces (1 1/2 cups) = 375 mL
16 fluid ounces (2 cups) = 500 mL

WEIGHTS (mass)

1/2 ounce = 15 g
1 ounce = 30 g
3 ounces = 90 g
4 ounces = 120 g
8 ounces = 225 g
10 ounces = 285 g
12 ounces = 360 g
16 ounces = 1 pound = 450 g

DIMENSIONS

1/16 inch = 2 mm
1/8 inch = 3 mm
1/4 inch = 6 mm
1/2 inch = 1.5 cm
3/4 inch = 2 cm
1 inch = 2.5 cm

OVEN TEMPERATURES

250°F = 120°C
275°F = 140°C
300°F = 150°C
325°F = 160°C
350°F = 180°C
375°F = 190°C
400°F = 200°C
425°F = 220°C
450°F = 230°C

BAKING PAN SIZES

Utensil	Size in Inches/Quarts	Metric Volume	Size in Centimeters
Baking or Cake Pan (square or rectangular)	8×8×2	2 L	20×20×5
	9×9×2	2.5 L	23×23×5
	12×8×2	3 L	30×20×5
	13×9×2	3.5 L	33×23×5
Loaf Pan	8×4×3	1.5 L	20×10×7
	9×5×3	2 L	23×13×7
Round Layer Cake Pan	8×1½	1.2 L	20×4
	9×1½	1.5 L	23×4
Pie Plate	8×1¼	750 mL	20×3
	9×1¼	1 L	23×3
Baking Dish or Casserole	1 quart	1 L	—
	1½ quarts	1.5 L	—
	2 quarts	2 L	—